Domestic Violence

and

OCCUPATION OF THE FAMILY HOME

Chris Bazell is Justices' Clerk for Northern Oxfordshire and joint Training Officer for Thames Valley. A solicitor, he is a former chair of the Justices' Clerks' Society Family Law Committee and Legal Adviser to the Magistrates' Association Family Proceedings Committee. He was a member of the Children Act Advisory Committee from 1994 to 1997 and in 1999 was seconded to work for the Judicial Studies Board to help develop human rights training for magistrates. He is co-author of *Introduction to the Family Proceedings Court* (1997).

Bryan Gibson is a barrister-at-law and was for 17 years a Clerk to the Justices in Hampshire — when he also served on the council of the Justices' Clerks' Society and as legal adviser to the Magistrates' Association Sentencing of Offenders Committee. He is a former co-editor of the weekly journal *Justice of the Peace* and now a full-time author and editor — and publisher of such works as *The Sentence of the Court* series (1996 to 1999), *Introduction to the Criminal Justice Process* (1995), *The Magistrates Bench Handbook* (1998) and *The Prisons Handbook* (1998).

Domestic Violence
and Occupation of the Family Home

Published 1999 by
WATERSIDE PRESS
Domum Road
Winchester SO23 9NN
Telephone or Fax 01962 855567
E-mail:watersidepress@compuserve.com

ISBN Paperback 1 872 870 60 0

Cataloguing-in-Publication Data A catalogue record for this book can be obtained from the British Library.

Printing and binding Antony Rowe Ltd, Chippenham.

Domestic Violence

and

OCCUPATION OF THE FAMILY HOME

Chris Bazell
Bryan Gibson

WATERSIDE PRESS
WINCHESTER

Preface

'Violence' and 'victims' have been very much to the forefront in recent years—or, in relation to the subject matter of this book, *domestic* violence and *survivors*, as victims of this particular type of violence have come to be described. As will be apparent from the text which follows there has been a great deal of activity on both these fronts—and we go to press as the government launches a concerted initiative to confront perpetrators of domestic violence and to ensure that survivors receive better, more sensitive and encouraging treatment than hitherto.

Essentially, this book sets out the law on domestic violence and the legal remedies which exist—but we have sought to do this against a backdrop of other relevant information. In summary our aim has been twofold:

- to explain the law as it applies to domestic violence; and

- to give background information which will allow people who deal with domestic violence perpetrators or survivors to carry out their responsibilities with a more rounded understanding than is provided by the letter of the law alone.

Law and practice

Indeed, it is doubtful whether *legal* remedies can ever themselves provide a complete answer to something which, at its base, is often bound up in personal and emotional considerations, the reality of which can remain hidden despite the use of formal powers. Nonetheless, it should be emphasised at the outset that there is now a strong momentum in favour of legal powers being used and of ensuring that incidents are not swept under the carpet. At the same time, mechanisms have emerged (some legal, some less formal) which, in practice, enhance the use of the law—or which avoid the need for it to be used by preventing offences and reducing future risks.

It is our view that judges, magistrates and the wide range of practitioners and volunteers who work in and around the criminal, civil and family courts need more than a knowledge of their own area of expertise. Each needs to be familiar with what the other is doing—so that all concerned can deal effectively with matters such as risk, safety, restraint, punishment, protection and welfare—the last item never more important than when children are involved. Fortunately, this is now the direction of government strategy as will emerge from the pages which follow.

Risk, danger, tensions and decision-making

There are ample indications in what follows that—once a domestic situation starts to deteriorate—the scope for escalation is unlimited, and practitioners should never underestimate the dangers. Even so, it should not be lost sight of that the vast majority of violent offenders are not qualitatively different to other people and *a fortiori*, perhaps, in a domestic context (though some perpetrators may have deep-seated psychological problems). There is always the potential for domestic violence even in the lives of ordinary people—whilst some domestic arrangements leave outsiders at a loss to understand why the remain intact at all, such are the conflicts and tensions. Whilst no-one should ever lose sight of the dangers it is conundrums of this kind with which judges, magistrates and other decision-makers are obliged to wrestle each day. If what we have written helps to advance this process in some small way then one of our central aims will have been achieved.

Scheme of *Domestic Violence and Occupation of the Family Home*

We have tried to provide as coherent an analysis as the subject matter permits. Following an introductory chapter which provides some information about the state of domestic violence and responses to it in Britain today, *Chapter 2* gives an overview of the main legal remedies—civil and criminal—for spouses, partners, children and other people who may be affected by violent domestic conflict. Domestic violence and other forms of unlawful personal interference are by no means restricted to adults, and we have included a more detailed outline of welfare considerations as they affect children—who may be primary victims of domestic violence or indirectly affected by it—in *Appendix II*.

These general protections are then developed in relation to areas where specialist knowledge is absolutely essential: non-molestation orders and occupation of the family home (*Chapter 3*), undertakings (*Chapter 4*), procedures (*Chapter 6*), enforcement of court orders (*Chapter 5*), and the innovative and, in our view, highly significant provisions on protection from harassment, including an explanation of the 'restraining order' and the unique twin track approach to *criminal* and *civil* relief (*Chapter 7*). Finally, in *Chapter 8*, we have tried to chart some *Strategies for Preventing Domestic Violence*, both before it occurs—which should be everyone's primary objective—or failing that before it can be repeated, thereby allowing us to return to some of those practical themes which it is our belief that every decision-maker should be acquainted with.

Chris Bazell and **Bryan Gibson**
July 1999

Domestic Violence
and Occupation of the Family Home

CONTENTS

Preface v

CHAPTER

Acknowledgements

Many people have contributed to this book by providing information, opinions and support and we are grateful to all of them. Our special thanks are due to the British Juvenile and Family Courts Society (BJFCS) for allowing us to study papers delivered at its international conference on Domestic Violence held in London in 1998, and to Maggie Silver, Winston Gordon, Peta Sissons, Robyn Holder, Peter Jeffries, Fiona Morton, Betsy Stanko, Sue Griffiths, Calvin Bell and Audrey Damazer.

Chris Bazell and **Bryan Gibson**
July 1999

CHAPTER 1

Introduction

In the summer of 1999 the government launched what it described as 'an integrated approach to tackling violence against women'. Included in this initiative were measures designed to protect women and children against domestic violence and similar forms of personal interference such as bullying and harassment. The priority now accorded to such matters is evident from the fact that this initiative occurred under the auspices of both the Cabinet Office and the Home Office. *Living Without Fear*[1] (the flagship publication for the venture) was launched jointly by Baroness Jay, minister for women, and Paul Boateng, minister of state at the Home Office. In her foreword, the former points out that

> Violence against women is a serious crime which this government is committed to tackling with vigour. Women have a right to live their lives without the fear of violence and mothers have the right to raise their children in safety . . . The sheer scale of violence and abuse has many dreadful consequences for individuals, families and the whole community.

Living Without Fear goes on to record the state of domestic violence in England and Wales towards the end of the twentieth century and notes the efforts being made to confront the phenomenon, including examples of good practice. Comparable initiatives have occurred in Scotland[2] and Northern Ireland[3]

DOMESTIC VIOLENCE AND THE LAW

As will be explained more fully in *Chapter 2, Law and Justice* when we look at the main legal remedies, there is no basic difference in law between *domestic* violence and violence *in any other context*. It is not as if there are special criminal offences or separate principles whereby domestic violence attains some enhanced status (as, in contrast, racially aggravated offences do pursuant to the Crime and Disorder Act 1998). An assault is an assault whenever and by whoever it is committed.

---

[1] *Living Without Fear: An Integrated Approach to Tackling Violence Against Women*, 1999, London: Cabinet Office/Home Office/COI (available from The Women's Unit, Cabinet Office, 2nd Floor, 10 George Street, London SW1 3AE). The Foreword is signed by Baroness Jay and Jack Straw, Home Secretary.

[2] *Preventing Violence Against Women: A Scottish Office Action Plan*, 1998

[3] *Tackling Violence Against Women: A Consultation Paper*, 1999

Neither are there any general exemptions which allow force to be used just because people are married or involved in some other relationship (the one exception concerns the lawful chastisement of children: see below). Often, the question is not one of law but of evidence or proof. As the government points out:

> What makes violence against women so hard to address is that women so often know their attackers and there are frequently no adult witnesses to these crimes. Many of them are committed in what should be the safety of a woman's home, even in front of children, by a partner to whom she should be able to look for support. These are dreadful violations of women and family life. To make matters worse, women often experience pressure and intimidation not to report the attack to the police or to help prosecute the offender. Not least for these reasons, we have been reluctant to face up to the seriousness of these crimes.[4]

Seriousness is again echoed when the government points out that 'Violent experiences can have damaging long-term consequences for women, including homelessness, physical and mental health problems, alcohol or drug abuse, and reduced employment opportunities'.[5] Thus, the criminal and civil remedies outlined in this book are not all simply referable to *physical* violence, but to other forms of personal interference—threats, abuse, menaces and harassment—which, quite apart from being unlawful in themselves, may escalate into physical assaults if not pre-empted. The remedies should be viewed as designed to prevent domestic violence, or to prevent it escalating. They should also be seen as protecting a wide range of people: spouses, partners, those in (or perhaps now out of) relationships, children and third parties. Our aim has been not only to explain what can be done to perpetrators but also to provide anyone facing or dealing with a deteriorating domestic situation—which could turn physically violent—with relevant legal and associated information.

Some special considerations
Despite the lack of any specific laws to deal with domestic violence, there *are* certain special considerations. To take examples from a wide range of items:

- some court orders are only available to specific categories of people who are linked by what (at this stage) can be described as domestic relationships or arrangements

---

4 *Living Without Fear*, p.6
5 Ibid, p.27

- in criminal proceedings there are legal rules about when one spouse can be compelled to give evidence against the other (a matter for more specialist advice)

- there is, in effect, a suspension of the normal context for offences during a marriage or relationship such that simply touching someone will not normally be viewed as assaultive behaviour nor every intimate advance as a prospective sexual assault—although a personal relationship, even marriage, does not confer any automatic rights (e.g. it remains an offence to use force on or rape a wife or partner, the ultimate issue usually being one of consent or otherwise)

- a parent may lawfully chastise a child within reason (although European obligations are increasingly limiting the scope for physical punishment or restraint: at the time of writing the UK is about to outlaw forms of physical punishment other than 'the open hand'. Many people would oppose even this.[6]

- civil courts (especially family courts) may adopt a less legalistic approach to problems which have a domestic context, e.g. when deciding whether to grant an injunction prohibiting certain conduct, a care order in respect of a child, or when regulating occupation of the family home.

It is also the case that—despite the lack of any uniquely targeted provisions—the remedies outlined in later chapters can, when used as part of a range of interventions, provide core protections: key measures for survivors or potential victims of domestic violence. These core protections are summarised later in this chapter under the heading *Dealing With Domestic Violence*.

THE EXTENT OF DOMESTIC VIOLENCE

The scale and impact of domestic violence in modern-day Britain can be judged, to some degree, by the size of the government's proposed investment: it has been announced that at least £6 million is to be made available from the Crime Reduction Programme to front-line agencies

---

[6] As this book went to press it was reported that a father without any previous blemish on his character had been held overnight in a police cell after he tried to restrain his 15 year old daughter from going out (to what he believed to be adverse influences) by grabbing her wrist. The daughter's charge of assault was later withdrawn.

tackling domestic violence, rape and sexual assault; that it is looking at providing 24 hour helplines for women; and that there is to be a staged increase in the grant to Victim Support to £19 million (up by £6.3 million). The government describes its overall goals as:

- in the long term, to reduce crimes of violence against women and the fear of violence

- to help today's children grow up in a society where violence is not part of family life and relationships are built on greater mutual respect; and

- within five years to see effective multi-agency partnerships operating throughout England and Wales, drawing on . . . good practice . . .

Good practice is a central theme of the government's commitment and it instances many examples from around the country. In a key passage from *Living Without Fear* it goes on to emphasise the scale of domestic violence, to point to past deficiencies in responses to survivors and to assure readers that the time has arrived for action:

> Violence against women is a serious crime with serious consequences. One in four women experience domestic violence at some stage in their lives. thousands of children live in fear in their own home, witnessing or experiencing violence . . . All across the UK, there are people working at the sharp end dealing with the consequences of violence against women. Volunteers, community organizations, probation officers, police, social workers and others have been working hard for many years to help and support women who experience violence. But help is still not comprehensive enough or easily accessible. In some cases, women are sent to up to ten different places before they get the help they need. And often how you are treated is entirely a matter of where you live. In some places, the service is extremely good and efficient; in others it simply does not exist . . . It is time to change that. We have moved on from the days when no one wanted to intervene in a domestic situation. Just as, as a society, we have woken up to the horrors of child abuse, it is time to act to change attitudes and make sure women are not subject to violence in their own home or anywhere else.[7]

The picture then, as this book goes to press, is of a serious and acknowledged social problem—but with 'no magic solutions'[8]—and a government which is determined to do something about it by:

---

[7] *Living Without Fear*, p.4
[8] Ibid, p.5

- providing timely support and protection ('Co-ordinated and effective help at the right time can save lives. Receiving timely help reduces the long-term consequences and helps to improve women's chances of a decent life'.)

- bringing perpetrators to justice ('The legal system must deter crimes of violence against women and provide support and protection for women pursuing cases through the courts'.)

- preventing violence ('Like other crimes, violence against women is unacceptable. Prevention is our long-term goal'.)

Some earlier findings

Many commentators would say that such action is long overdue. The scale of domestic violence has been known and understood for some time and a range of interest groups have pressed government with the view that responses and facilities have been inadequate. In the early 1990s, a swathe of 'Key Research Findings' were assembled by Robyn Holder and Peta Sissons of the independent consultancy Awareness in Practice[9] who were compelled, at the time, to comment that

> . . . there has been no national prevalence study of domestic violence conducted in the UK, nor are figures collected by the Home Office from police a true or accurate picture of the level of incidence. However . . . *local* studies . . . give a detailed picture of a very serious crime problem (emphasis added).

Assessing the impact of domestic violence by reference to such information and statistics (often localised) as did then exist demonstrated, e.g. that:

- ninety-eight to ninety-nine per cent of domestic violence was committed by men against women with whom they were or had been in a relationship (Metropolitan Police)

- one in five of all murder victims was a woman killed by a current or former partner (Home Office),

---

[9] *Awareness in Practice: Understanding Domestic Violence Key Research Findings,* Robyn Holder and Peta Sissons, 1994. This survey was developed for training purposes and presented at the British Juvenile and Family Courts Society international conference on Domestic Violence held in London in 1997. Full references are contained in *Challenging Domestic Violence,* Hammersmith and Fulham Community Safety Unit, 1991. We are grateful to both the BJFCS and the authors for their assistance.

- domestic violence was the largest category of murder in the Metropolitan Police District (Home Affairs Select Committee, 1993)

- 28 per cent of women had suffered physical injury from their partners in their lifetime (Mooney, 1993)

- violence usually escalates in severity and frequency over time to about two attacks per woman per week (Dobash and Dobash, 1984; Walker, 1977).

The government's own conclusion with regard to its current Crime Reduction Programme is that

> Domestic violence is the largest single form of violent crime against women. Under the Crime and Disorder Act 1998, local crime audits are required to identify the nature and prevalence of all crime locally, including crimes such as domestic violence which are often not reported, and therefore not recorded by the police. Local partnerships are required to devise strategies to reduce crime and disorder in their area. A number have identified domestic violence as their top priority.

Indeed, on the known information, domestic violence is probably far more commonplace and wide-ranging than is often realised—and even what *is* known may represent but a fraction of the incidents which occur. Under-reporting to the authorities of events which occur behind closed doors seems to be a truism; the real extent of domestic violence can never be known. However, what *is* known is that domestic violence occurs across a broad cross-section of the population. In another paper written for the British Juvenile and Family Courts Society (BJFCS), Peter Jeffries of the Inner London Probation Service commented:

> The [Probation] Service has always been aware of the high levels of violence and intimidation which regularly exist in proceedings involving separation and divorce. The extent of that violence and its location around child contact matters has been highlighted by researchers, as have the effects of violence on children. That research and the recent implementation of the domestic violence provisions in the Family Law Act 1996 have focused the attention of Family Court Welfare Officers [a branch of the Probation Service] on the very real risks run by many women and children after they have separated from their partners. [10]

---

[10] Peter Jeffries, Assistant Chief Probation Officer, 'Domestic Violence and Probation in the United Kingdom', 1997: British Juvenile and Family Courts Society/Inner London Probation Service.

The Inner London Probation Service has since developed and now operates a range of provision for perpetrators and survivors as outlined in *Chapter 8*.

Other findings about domestic violence

The 'Key Research Findings' above are again instructive in drawing attention to the *level* of domestic violence as it has existed for some time. Thus of the more memorable and striking statistics:

- violence occurs in between 10 to 30 per cent of heterosexual relationships (Kelly, 1988; Dobash and Dobash, 1992)

- 48 per cent of women experience verbal or physical threats from a household member or male partner and 30 per cent of women have been physically assaulted at least once by a partner/household member (McGibbon *et al*, 1989)

- one in three of all recorded offences of violence against women was domestic violence (Home Office, 1989)

- one in eight women have been raped by their husbands or partners (Painter, 1991)

- an estimated three quarters of a million incidents of domestic violence occur in London each year (London Strategic Policy Unit, 1986).

The government's figures

The absence of a nationwide profile has, to some extent, been remedied by information contained in *Living Without Fear* and other documents and sources referred to in that publication.[11] Thus the government notes, among other things, that:

- one woman in four experiences domestic violence at some stage in her life and it is estimated that between one in eight and one in ten has experienced domestic violence in the past year (*British Crime Survey*, 1998)

- every week two women are killed by their current or former partners (*Homicide Statistics*, 1998)

---

[11] *Living Without Fear*, see footnote 1. Whilst there is now something in the nature of nationwide profile there are those who would question the reliability of the *British Crime Survey* to give a fully accurate picture of the extent of domestic violence: though valuable, it is essentially impressionistic rather than scientific.

- every day thousands of children witness cruelty and violence behind closed doors. More than a third of children of domestic violence survivors are aware of what is going on and this rises to a half if the woman has suffered repeat violence (*British Crime Survey*, 1998)

- domestic violence accounts for one quarter of all violent crime (*British Crime Survey*, 1998)

- women aged 16 to 29 are at the greatest risk of experiencing domestic violence (*British Medical Association Review*, 1998)

- domestic violence often starts or escalates during pregnancy (*British Medical Association Review*, 1998).

Investment in tackling domestic violence is thus more than justified. Among the projects to attract a share of the additional £6 million funding referred to earlier in this chapter are those involving: training for the judiciary, the police and Crown Prosecution Service; improving evidence gathering techniques (*Chapter 2*); enhanced databases (e.g. concerning women's refuges (*Chapter 3*); multi-agency working (see later in this chapter and *Chapter 8*); education and prevention programmes and a range of work with offenders (*Chapter 8*). As to multi-agency working, it is within an integrated framework that the government aims '. . . to disseminate to those at the sharp end practical information, ideas and contacts, to secure consistent and effective help for the female victims of violence across the country'.

The inadequacy of responses
There is—as the government has since acknowledged in general terms in *Living Without Fear*—a substantial question mark over whether responses to domestic violence are adequate, albeit there are indications, e.g. that police, prosecutors and others involved in the justice system and key support agencies are increasingly more likely to act, listen, respond, and treat complainants and witnesses sympathetically and in more appropriate ways than hitherto.

DEALING WITH DOMESTIC VIOLENCE

Notwithstanding the lack of specific laws to deal with domestic violence as noted earlier in this chapter there are certain key legal measures which are (or become) particularly significant in the domestic context and which serve as core protections.

The core protections

The items listed below form the central focus of this book and are discussed within the following framework, together with extracts from key statutory provisions and, where we believe that it will assist understanding of complex areas, key forms and other relevant materials:

- the many general protections under the criminal law and the civil law: *Chapter 2*

- non-molestation orders and occupation of the family home: *Chapter 3*

- court undertakings to refrain from particular conduct or to do certain things: *Chapter 4*

- the relatively recent law on protection from harassment: *Chapter 7*

- measures designed to ensure the welfare of children (including the longstanding 'welfare principle' which is a constant theme in this respect): *Appendix II.*

Ultimately, it is a sound knowledge of all the above items (and in many cases how court orders are enforced: *Chapter 6*) which enables an informed decision to be made in any given situation. Choices abound, from the deceptively simple one whether to pursue civil or criminal remedies (or both) through to which route to follow, e.g. should it be a claim of non-molestation under the family jurisdiction or an allegation of harassment in either the criminal or civil courts. The chapters which follow are intended not only to describe the various remedies, but to enable readers to assess the pros and cons.[12]

THE COST OF DOMESTIC VIOLENCE

Quite apart from considerations of how women survivors and child survivors should be treated there is the quite separate question of how much domestic violence costs in financial terms. Whilst there is still—so far as we are aware—no nationwide assessment of these costs it is not difficult to point to a range of items for inclusion in any account, starting with the cost of the emergency services, court proceedings and imprisonment and ending with the impact on the physical and emotional

---

[12] It is also interesting to note Eliabeth Burney's findings concerning efforts by social landlords to counter domestic violence and other 'anti-social behaviour' via contractual terms inserted into contracts to occupy property: see *Crime and Banishment: Nuisance and Exclusion in Social Housing*, Waterside Press, 1999.

health of survivors, not just at the time of the events but often for many years ahead. Betwixt and between there are all manner of community costs including those which fall on the education and housing services. It is thus somewhat imprecise (and maybe something of an understatement) when the government says that 'Supporting women survivors is already costing millions of pounds' although it does acknowledge such published research as does exists, e.g. that the cost is £278 million per year in Greater London alone which

> . . . did not include the costs of prosecuting offenders or the costs associated with domestic homicide . . . and many [of the overall] costs are borne by organizations at the sharp end—providing emergency forms of help to women in crisis.[13]

The financial costs aspect of domestic violence is one reason why the government is investing sums of the order mentioned earlier in this chapter—with a view to reducing expense and inefficiency, the view being that as progress is made resources will then be released for more proactive, preventative work of the kind which we outline in *Chapter 8*.[14]

THE RANGE OF DOMESTIC VIOLENCE

The prevailing image of domestic violence is the *physical* assault, usually *by a man* on a women (the so-called 'battered wife/partner'). But this is misleading: such conduct can take many forms. The law—including the criminal law—has recognised increasingly that violence does not just mean physical violence in the conventional sense of someone hitting or battering someone else (*Chapter 2*). The form which violence takes and its degree or extent will in turn dictate which of the remedies described in this book can be—or ought to be—sought. In *Counting the Costs*,[15] Betsy Stanko and her colleagues explain that:

> Domestic violence is a generic term which refers to abusive and assaultive behaviour between intimates, among members of a household, and/or between former partners. Its most dominant form is man to woman within a partnership or former partnership . . .

> Domestic violence also exists within some same sex relationships.

---

[13] *Living Without Fear*, p.8. The Hackney costs are detailed in *Counting the Costs: Estimating the Impact of Domestic Violence in the London Borough of Hackney*, Betsy Stanko *et al*, Crime Concern/Safer Cities/The Children's Society, 1998. Two measures/estimates were used: key agencies (£189m); total costs (£278m).

[14] *Living Without Fear*, p.8

[15] *Counting the Cost*, see footnote 13.

Taking this definition, the authors explain that 'abusive behaviour' would include a variety of words, actions or ill-treatment, whilst 'assaultive behaviour' would extend to any form of unwarranted physical interference (including sexual interference or harassment). All these items can fall within the reach of the law, provided they satisfy certain criteria outlined in later chapters. As Stanko *et al* observe:

> Psychological abuse (for example, constant criticism, domineering or threatening behaviour), physical and sexual assault, as well as acting in controlling ways over household decision-making and finances, all intertwine with family and sexual intimacies. What constitutes domestic violence varies from individual to individual, as do the legal, economic and psychological consequences which serve to keep people entangled within abusive and violent relationships.

Thus, domestic violence may encompass a very wide range of *criminal* behaviour: see generally *Chapter 2*. But, equally, there are other *non-criminal* aspects—and common traits which the same authors describe as follows:

> Being under constant and severe criticism, belittled and demeaned, given no money to feed and/or clothe oneself and one's children and made to feel worthless may have no 'criminal' referent, but [they] are debilitating nonetheless . . . What is common to all domestic violence is fear: fear of being harmed further; fear of death; fear of having the children taken away if assistance is sought; fear of not being able to find any place safe to live; fear of being without a loved one (even if he is the one who is doing the frightening); fear that leaving will not remove the threat of retaliation; fear of being seen as a failure by not keeping intimate relationships happy and healthy.

Some of these items would now properly fall under the Protection From Harassment Act 1997, which is designed to prevent a course of conduct which puts someone in fear of violence or threats of violence, or which wrongly interferes with another person's legitimate interests: *Chapter 7*. Likewise, certain such behaviour will amount to molestation within the meaning of the Family Law Act 1996: *Chapter 3*. Just as a broader range of actions are nowadays recognised as amounting to unlawful personal interference the legal remedies have tended to embrace a wider range of relationships and scenarios than hitherto.

Avoiding myths and stereotyping

The stereotype of domestic violence as an integral part of working-class existence is misleading (and probably always was). Thus the 'Key Research Findings' already mentioned note that

> . . . Battered women come from all walks of life. Social class, family income, level of education, occupation, and ethnic or religious background make little difference. (Smith, 1989)

A similar wariness is required in respect of other myths such as: men who abuse were abused as children (indeed, much work with offenders now disregards the perpetrator's own history, as opposed to the history of his offences, as a largely irrelevant consideration); domestic violence is mainly alcohol related (as many crimes are, but not such that offenders are excused or treated differently); domestic violence is more brutal in Asian families; and if the violence were truly as bad as all that the woman would quite obviously leave (which raises questions about the dilemmas of dependence and controlling behaviour mentioned later in this chapter, and the overall 'cycle of abuse' mentioned in *Chapter 8*). As Davina James-Hanman, co-ordinator of the Greater London Domestic Violence Project pointed out in 1997:

> . . . each misunderstanding and stereotype needs to be exposed and corrected before attitudes, and subsequently practice, will change. For example, if police officers believe that women will always withdraw charges, this affects their willingness to arrest. If court clerks believe that leaving a relationship will end violence, the necessary steps are not taken to maintain security measures such as keeping new addresses confidential. If judges and magistrates believe that men are violent when they lose control, rather than it being a deliberate and intentional act, anger management courses may seem to be a reasonable intervention rather than dangerous and potentially lethal.[16]

She identifies from her own experience a lack of knowledge and understanding across the system. She also points to policy and practice gaps and a general lack of co-ordination 'which means that a woman may have to make between five and 12 contacts before getting the help required' (a complaint since adopted, accepted and emphasised in *Living Without Fear*). She goes on to identify a starting point for legal personnel involving:

- comprehensive training for all legal staff and attendance at their local domestic violence inter-agency forum

- prioritising women and children's safety within the legal process, i.e. ensuring new addresses are not revealed, having somewhere safe to wait before court appearances, etc

---

[16] Davina James-Hanman, 'Domestic Violence: Current Issues', London: BJFCS, 1997; and see *What Support?: A Study of Local Services*, McGibbon *et al*, 1989.

- better collation of evidence before sentencing such as routinely asking the Probation Service for pre-sentence reports (PSRs)

- using interventions which have been proven to be most effective in stopping abusive men from re-offending, i.e. not imposing fines but, e.g. imprisonment or making orders requiring abusive men to attend re-education programmes

- more careful consideration of applications for residency or contact orders to take account of the impact on children (and women) of ruling in favour of men

- assistance in minimising the effects of cuts in legal aid by developing an easy-to-use system for women to make their own applications for non-molestation and occupation orders.

FEARS AND DILEMMAS

We have already intimated that a woman may continue in a domestic violence situation from fear or bewilderment ('He's bound to come after me'; 'How will I survive financially'; 'He's basically quite nice—he promised me the world if I would stay'). There are, indeed, many such traps. Is it a one-off incident? Is the perpetrator really like this? There may also be confused loyalties wrought out of the fact that the individuals became involved with each other to start with so that a natural, if perverse, reaction may be to make excuses and cover-up—and a survivor's self-esteem is hardly enhanced if she is being belittled or made to feel that it is *her* fault a relationship has gone wrong. Modern thinking is that reducing patterns of domestic violence involves an inter-agency response which makes it safe for women to seek help, provides support and encouragement of the kind described in *Chapter 8*, and which shifts the onus from the woman to the authorities.

Several commentators have referred to what they identify as a 'cycle of abuse'. For instance, that in use by the Everyman Centre in Plymouth which provides psycho-social counselling for men perpetrators (see further at *Chapter 8*) identifies the 'serial or cyclical batterer' as someone who starts blaming and accusing, dominates and controls, violently assaults, apologises, shows remorse, expresses his guilt and makes promises, sulks and withdraws getting edgy and withdraws affection—following which the blaming and accusing begins all over again. At various points in this cycle, the victim may be in shock, need to cope with pleas for forgiveness, morbid jealousy if she dresses up or goes out, a heightening of inner tensions and a variety of threats, sarcasm, ridicule and humiliation. Expectations may be challenged if the survivor asserts any form of independence or disobedience, when anger can be quickly expressed so as to re-assert control and reduce the anxiety felt as a result of perceived rejection. Conversely, the survivor may try to take control of the time and place of the beatings. Understanding domestic violence requires a recognition of this possible sub-text; and careful probing to ensure that twisted loyalties do not mask the seriousness of what is happening or prevent appropriate interventions to ensure the safety of all concerned.

CHILDREN AND THIRD PARTIES

It is often the case that a third party gets caught up in a domestic violence situation (albeit that the chief intensity of any attack or emotional onslaught is invariably directed towards the other party to a marriage, relationship or one time relationship).[17] Third parties such as relatives, friends and associates are protected by the general law— criminal or civil—relevant aspects of which have been widened in recent years. Thus, e.g. the non-molestation provisions and those affecting occupation of the family home apply to 'associated' persons as defined in the Family Law Act 1996. Injunctions under both the 1996 Act and the Protection From Harassment Act 1997, and retraining orders under the latter, can name third parties who are not to be interfered with (see, generally, *Chapters 3* and *7*), as can court undertakings (*Chapter 4*).

Children are also often caught in an impossible misplaced fear-cum-loyalty-cum-dependence trap. They may be effected either because they are bystanders witnessing violence on or by a parent, or they may be primary victims. They automatically enjoy the protection of any special third party legal protections discussed in other chapters, but are also covered by direct provisions ranging from those criminal offences designed to protect people below a certain age (including special measures concerning sexual assaults) to the care and emergency protection measures contained in the Children Act 1989. These special protections are summarised in *Chapter 2* and welfare considerations expanded upon in *Appendix II*.

Betsy Stanko *et al* (above) note that it is nowadays accepted that domestic violence '. . . is common amongst any general population of women [such that] . . . Its impact goes beyond the suffering of individual women, and also involves that of their children, their social and friendship support, and the wider networks of their (and their assailant's) families'.

---

[17] In the case of harassment that 'relationship' may be one-sided—or even imaginary

The decision to include in this book an outline of the special protections afforded to children also seems to be vindicated by *Living Without Fear* where the government notes that

> Domestic violence scars the lives of many children. More than a third of the children of domestic violence survivors are aware of what is going on — this rises to 45 per cent if the woman has suffered repeat violence. Depression, anxiety, hyperactivity, eating problems, heightened aggression, difficulties with concentration and stress-related illnesses such as asthma and bronchitis, are all short or long-term effects on children witnessing violence.[18]

It is also supported by 'Key Research Findings'[19] such as the following:

- children in violent households witness and/or experience the violence in 50 per cent of instances (Stark and Flitcraft, 1988)

- 66 per cent of residents in emergency refuges are children (Women's Aid)

- in one of two to three cases of domestic violence, child abuse is also occurring (Stark and Flitcraft, 1988).

As with women survivors, child abuse is likely to be under-reported, due to the very nature of the family situation and the fact that the younger the child the more likely he or she is to assume that their parents know best; and through isolation within the family that this, in effect, is how life is supposed to be. The same confused loyalty factors which contribute to under-reporting of assaults on women are likely to be writ large in the case of a child. Loyalty, secrecy, shame and low self-esteem may serve to reinforce one another in the covering up process.

Naturally, there are major hurdles for a child bent on reporting matters. These include the 'normalisation' of behaviour within a family setting, fear of reprisals, a general lack of power, fear of the unknown and fear of what might happen to the adult concerned. Increasingly, the danger to some children has been recognised, to wit the existence of local authority 'At-risk registers' in which many agencies participate in terms of supplying information for oversight by a Local Review Committee and the proliferation of helplines and counsellors. There is, of course, the problem that someone along this chain has to recognise the key signs and children usually tend only to be classified as at-risk when corroborative signals flow from two or more agencies. A number of high

---

[18] *Living Without Fear,* p.28
[19] See footnote 9

profile cases where the signs of abuse were only discerned with the benefit of hindsight have demonstrated just how difficult getting behind the 'family facade' can become—and emphasised the need for vigilance.

Again, dealing with 'popular mythology', there is no hard evidence to suggest that abused women are more likely to have witnessed/experienced violence as children.

Some further points affecting children from *Living Without Fear* can also be conveniently noted at this point (quite apart from the effects which domestic violence witnessed by a child can have on him or her):

- the government's plans involve a review of funding for child contact centres (i.e. neutral places where contact between a parent and child can take place in safety vis-à-vis both the mother and child) and conducting research into the outcome of child contact arrangements.

- the risk of conflict arising from child contact arrangements which involve handing over or visiting a child at the woman's home is high, so that neutral meeting places in a supported environment— with volunteers to facilitate such meetings—are critical in those cases where the delicate balance of welfare considerations re the child indicates that conduct with a parent who may have abused the mother or the child should be maintained.

- a nationwide charity, the National Association of Child Contact Centres supports over 250 centres across Britain, encourages new projects, develops consistent standards and provides training for those involved in this work.[20]

We did not think it appropriate in a book dealing primarily with domestic violence against women to feature those specialist and well-known initiatives such as Childline and Children in Need which provide a lifeline and support for children who are being abused by adults—but their existence and work should nonetheless be noted.

---

[20] Ibid, pp.11 and 40.

WOMEN'S AID, ASSISTANCE AND SUPPORT

There are now refuges in most parts of the country where women can find temporary respite and a means of escape from violence. Indeed, *Living Without Fear* notes that there are some 400 in England and 45 in Wales (July 1999). Here, women who are fleeing violence can find safe accommodation and services that give them physical protection, confidentiality, support and advice to help them deal with the situation they find themselves in. The refuge movement was established largely by the voluntary sector and it remains independent of government:

> Women can use refuge accommodation as a breathing space while they plan what to do next. Some will decide to pursue legal remedies such as injunctions and/or exclusion orders so that they can return home. Those unable or unwilling to return home for fear of further violence will need alternative accommodation.[21]

There are several key players, including the umbrella organization Women's Aid and the nationwide charity Refuge. We discuss this important aspect of protection for women in greater detail in *Chapter 3* which also deals among other things with what can frequently be related issues: preventing molestation and occupation of the family home.

DOMESTIC VIOLENCE AGAINST MEN

As Betsy Stanko *et al* point out concerning domestic violence: 'Its most dominant form is man to woman'.[22] The evidence from local studies, police statistics and from a wide range of agencies confirm that in by far the majority of instances and reports of domestic violence, the violence was carried out by men against their women partners or ex-partners.

However, violence against men by partners (male and female) does take place. A report in 1993 indicated between three per cent and ten per cent of domestic violence was committed against men, and a later *British Crime Survey* reported in 1998[23] that 15 per cent of men aged 16 to 59 said they had been physically assaulted by a current or former partner at

---

[21] Ibid. p.23

[22] *Counting the Costs:* see footnote 13. The authors acknowledge relying on information in that work in parts of this section.

[23] *Domestic Violence: Findings From the BCS Self-Completion Questionnaire,* Home Office Research Findings No. 86, 1998. Women's Aid Federation England have published a critique of the BCS report and the way the press reported it (*WAFE Newsletter,* June 1999).

some point in their lives. However, further examination of that report shows that

> ... men are less often injured than women, are considerably less frightened and are less likely to seek medical help. Women are disproportionately affected by certain forms of violent crime and the fear of crime.

Other studies indicate that something like three per cent up to ten per cent of domestic violence is by partners or ex-partners, female or male, on men (e.g. LHU, 1993). The situation is thus not wholly one of man-on-women violence. The law has had to come to terms with a proliferation of (now increasingly open) same sex relationships—as well as that minority of heterosexual relationships in which the woman has attacked a male partner. Vera Baird, a barrister, identified cases where

> ... women who have suffered domestic violence ... for a protracted period ... eventually turn on their persecutor and kill him ... Often this is done after years and frequently the death is caused by a single blow such as a stab with a kitchen knife.[24]

Quite often, defences to murder of diminished responsibility or provocation are put forward (neither of which completely displaces responsibility: both serve to reduce the offence to one of manslaughter): see, generally, for criminal offences, *Chapter 2.*

If domestic violence on women is grossly unreported, under-reporting of violence on men, especially when it is committed by women, is perhaps even greater. This is likely to centre around a belief that admitting they have been attacked is admitting to some kind of failing as a man—an indication that they are incapable of defending themselves. If so, they do not fit society's pre-conceived notion of their sex role. By contrast, a woman suffering violence, though she may have other powerful reasons for being reluctant to report it, is unlikely be deterred by the prospect that if people know that she has been a victim of violence they will think her unfeminine. Furthermore, there may often be a difference in quality when it comes to violence on men.

For some 20 years, family law legislation has not sought to make any fundamental distinction between the rights of men and women in relation to the home, finances or children. The criminal law makes few distinctions, and largely where this is inherent in the physical difference between the sexes. A striking example of discrimination is that the age of consent in a gay relationship is 18, in a heterosexual one 16. Political pressure meant that government attempts to bring the former into line

---

[24] Vera Baird, 'Battered Women Who Kill: An Outline of Some Recent Cases and the Current State of the Law', *BJFCS Newsletter,* July 1998.

with the latter in the Crime and Disorder Act 1998 meant that the relevant clauses had to be abandoned.

Seemingly, harassment (see, generally, *Chapter 7*) of men by women is not uncommon, or so the anecdotal evidence of day-to-day court experience and the occasional press reports suggest.

A DIVERSE PROBLEM

This overview indicates the diverse nature of domestic violence and its quite substantial, everyday impact on many families. It also highlights the need for sound training of and an understanding of the issues by all concerned, the co-ordination and effectiveness of both formal and informal responses to domestic violence and a continuing need to dispel myths and misunderstandings. Only then is it possible to make sense of the wide range of legal provision and case law, civil and criminal, with which domestic violence can be addressed. It is instructive to close this introduction with a summary of what government has promised to do as we approach the new millennium. In essence, it describes the approach as built around three pillars as follows:

- protection and provision—women need to know they can find the support they need, when and where they need it;

- justice—the legal system needs to deter crime and provide support and protection for women pursuing cases through the courts; and

- prevention—like other crimes, prevention is our long-term goal.

A note about what is being done—or in some instances what will be done or is proposed—is incorporated into later chapters where appropriate. Central features are multi-agency strategies, integrated local schemes (including inter-agency partnerships) and the 'one stop shop' approach—all of which have proved their worth in other areas of criminal justice. At ministerial level the essential co-operation is emphasised by the wide inter-departmental nature of the government's 1999 initiative[22] and the fact that it is scheduled to be developed by what is described as a 'cross-cutting unit at the Home Office'. The initiative is also fuelled by a strong awareness of past deficiencies:

---

[22] The participants in the Interdepartmental Steering Group were: the Crown Prosecution Service, Department for Education and Employment, Department of Health, Department of the Environment, Transport and the Regions, Department of Social Security, Health and Safety Executive, Home Office, Lord Chancellor's Department, National Assembly for Wales and the Women's Unit at the Cabinet Office

Whenever and wherever a woman seeks help, the professionals need to be alert to the possibility that she may have been assaulted and to guide her to the help she needs. Police, local authorities, health services and voluntary organizations should encourage women to report sexual and domestic violence.[23]

In an effort to ensure that women do in future receive a positive response, it is urged, for example, that the relevant agencies consider:

- publicity campaigns, such as leaflets, posters and press coverage, to increase awareness of services and encourage women to come forward;

- routine questioning about sexual and domestic violence in areas such as health and mental health to encourage earlier identification of violence as an underlying cause of problems; and

- well-advertised complaints procedures so that women can feel confident that any difficulties they encounter will be taken seriously.

One element of the awareness programme is the government's own *Break the Chain* leaflet and supporting posters. This campaign, launched in January 1999 aims to raise awareness that domestic violence *is* a crime, to inform survivors about a range of relevant matters and later on to target perpetrators, professionals who deal with survivors and the community at large. The leaflet itself seeks to offer practical advice and sources of help, encourages women to recognise what is happening rather than to blame themselves, and to seek help and support.[24] It is when domestic violence is diagnosed or when women do seek that help that information of the kind contained in the remainder of this book becomes all important.

---

[23] *Living Without Fear,* p.16

[24] Copies of this leaflet which includes a pull-out section the size of a credit card with useful telephone numbers and space to enter those of local agencies can be obtained from the Home Office by telephoning 0171 273 4145 (Fax 0171 273 2568).

CHAPTER 2

Law and Justice

As we noted in *Chapter 1* justice in the sense of an effective and supportive legal system is one of the three pillars of government strategy in relation to domestic violence. This chapter provides an overview of the main legal protections as well as indicating the difference between *criminal* and *civil* remedies, the latter subdivided into those under the general law and those under the family jurisdiction. It can be noted at the outset that the emphasis in initiatives such as *Break the Chain* (see p.28) is that domestic violence is first and foremost a criminal offence. It is worth repeating here the following words from *Living Without Fear:*

> Domestic violence is the largest single form of violent crime against women. Under the Crime and Disorder Act 1998, local crime audits are required to identify the nature and prevalence of all crime locally, including crimes such as domestic violence . . . A number have identified domestic violence as their top priority.[1]

There are situations where resort to the civil law may be more appropriate, as e.g. when harassment is connected with other proceedings before the civil courts or where occupation of the family home is in issue. It is also the case that the civil law concept of 'molestation' may be wider than conduct caught by the criminal law and the standard of proof is lower in civil proceedings. But criminal proceedings are not pre-empted simply because civil proceedings are contemplated. Thus the same events could be the subject matter of any or all of the following:

- a criminal prosecution; and/or
- a civil action; and/or
- an application before the family courts, where the same behaviour forms the basis, say, a divorce petition.[2]

---

[1] *Living Without Fear,* p.13. See page 9 of this work for details of that publication.

[2] In 1999 the government changed its mind about a comprehensive move to 'no fault' divorce. Naturally, there can be no overlap between civil and family proceedings if one or other court has exclusive jurisdiction as with some remedies described in this book. But there is nothing in principle to prevent, say, a criminal charge of assault, a civil action for damages for that assault and a divorce based principally upon unreasonable, i.e. assaultive, behaviour (or the same behaviour might affect the financial arrangements following divorce).

It can also be noted that the conduct of parents, criminal or otherwise, may affect the basis for care proceedings in respect of children and decisions by courts and local authorities concerning the future welfare of children.

Formal responses

The extent to which the legal system has—historically speaking—been called upon to respond to incidents of domestic violence can be judged from a selection of the 'Key Research Findings' assembled by Robyn Holder and Peta Sissons:[3]

- 25 per cent of all violent crime reported to police is domestic violence (Dobash, 1979)

- 25 per cent of recorded serious assault in the Metropolitan Police District is domestic violence, which is the largest category of assaults (HASC, 1993)

- over 1,500 calls for help are made to the London Metropolitan Police per week (est 1991: 37,000 calls to attend)

- 15,000 protection orders (since replaced by non-molestation orders under the Family Law Act 1996: *Chapter 3*) were granted by the courts in England and Wales in 1988 (Barron, 1992)

- 1,500 domestic incidents were reported to police in one London division in one year of which two thirds were reported as criminal allegations (Edwards, 1989).

According to the government's own assessment such crimes can be complicated, e.g. by virtue of a relationship between victim and perpetrator; the lack of adult witnesses; the consequent difficulty in obtaining evidence; and fear of the justice process—and as we have already commented in *Chapter 1* the question may not simply be whether an offence is committed, recognised as an offence or recorded as such but one of evidence, proof, fear of retaliation and the general dilemma which exists where a man has control of the domestic situation. Nonetheless increasing numbers of women *are* reporting violent crimes to statutory and voluntary organizations even if there remains significant under-reporting:

> The number of rapes recorded by police has increased more than three-fold between 1985 and 1997, mainly as a result of the welcome increase in the

---

[3] *Awareness in Practice:* see p.13 of this work for full details of that publication.

reporting of acquaintance and intimate rapes. In spite of this, there is still significant under-reporting . . . Similarly, only 17 per cent of people who identified themselves as a survivor of a domestic assault said that the police were aware of one or more incidents in the previous year.[4]

One initiative which will in future encourage reporting is the introduction of more helplines. These enable women to reach professional assistance whether emergency services or for the purposes e.g. of counselling. The government's commitment in this regard is to the development of a 24 hour service nationwide for what it describes, literally, as 'lifelines', citing as an example of good practice the Women's Aid National Domestic Violence Helpline.[5]

Criminal Proceedings

Crime reduction is one of the government's overall goals—something first given statutory expression in the Crime and Disorder Act 1998 and now the pre-fix for virtually every statement of criminal policy. It is as an integral part of the government's Crime Reduction Programme that it has decided to invest 'at least 6 million' to address domestic violence and other crimes against women in what are described as 'innovative projects that will make a difference'.

It would not be appropriate in a book of this nature to dwell upon the basics of criminal law or its general principles in that cases of domestic violence have precisely the same status as any other criminal matter and are dealt with—without any legal differentiation in the nature of the charge or charges—by the Crown Court or magistrates' court according to standard procedures. However, this ought not to obscure the many real and substantive differences which can exist regarding such allegations as alluded to in *Chapter 1*. Moreover, the sheer scale of criminal protections cannot be ignored and we have tried to list the main offences which are likely to be encountered below.

The classification of criminal offences, i.e. whether they are 'purely summary', 'triable either way' or 'indictable only' determines their progress—together, in the case of either way offences, with decisions made at the preliminary stage of the proceedings concerning whether the case should be tried by magistrates or by a jury and, where a guilty plea is indicated at the outset, whether sentence for such an offence should be

---

[4] *Domestic Violence: Findings From a New British Crime Survey Self-completion Questionnaire*, Research Study No 191, Home Office, 1999

[5] *Living Without Fear*, p.20

passed by magistrates or at Crown Court within its greater powers.[6] What is certain is that the fact that violence occured in a domestic context will not serve to lessen the gravity of the offences involved.

Criminal offences

If death occurs following an assault or as a consequence of violent events a charge of murder or manslaughter will normally result. A conviction for manslaughter may result from a reduction of the charge where. e.g. the defendant successfully claims diminished responsibility or provocation: legally speaking, there is no equivalent in the United Kingdom to the french *crime passionnel*. Of the very many lesser criminal offences which may figure in a domestic context are the following:

- causing grievous bodily harm with intent (section 18 Offences Against the Person Act 1861)

- malicious wounding (section 20 of the 1861 Act)

- assault occasioning actual bodily harm (section 47 of the 1861 Act)

- rape, unlawful sexual intercourse, indecent assault, gross indecency (and a range of sexual offences).

- kidnapping or abduction

- blackmail

- threats to kill someone whether orally or in writing

- harassment (new offences, powers and legal remedies were created in 1997: *Chapter 7*)

- a range of public order and nuisance type offences including all those outlined separately for the purposes of comparison with harassment in *Chapter 7*

- theft and fraud. There are a wide range of potential offences. In the case of the Theft Act 1998 some of these involve violent ingredients which may well feature in a domestic situation, as with robbery

---

[6] Usually more than six months per either way offence or 12 months in aggregate. See, generally, *The Sentence of the Court*, Michael Watkins *et al*, Waterside Press, 1998; *Introduction to the Magistrates' Court*, Bryan Gibson, Waterside Press, 1999.

and certain forms of aggravated burglary. Breaking into a house, e.g. with intent to rape falls within this last mentioned offence.

- criminal damage, e.g. breaking down a door or tearing up or destroying clothes, or damaging personal belongings

- arson (criminal damage by fire)

- obstructing the course of justice, e.g. by interfering with witnesses, giving false or misleading information

- perjury by lying on oath in court or when swearing an affidavit

- wasting police time.

Criminal offences may be committed not only in relation to adults, but also vis-à-vis children who may also need protection via a court order: see *Child Protection In Outline* later in this chapter.

Escalation

It is also possible for relatively minor offences to escalate rapidly into much more serious ones as noted in *Chapter 1*. Not only, e.g. might verbal harassment turn into physical violence, but any violence is intrinsically dangerous. Given some flashpoint, a minor rift can lead to danger in seconds. A conspiracy by two or more people to commit a criminal offence is also a very serious matter, as where family members 'gang up on' the survivor or, in the extreme (but seemingly by no means that unusual) situation where a partner puts out a 'contract'. Similarly, people may become involved as secondary parties, i.e. as aiders and abettors, or because they have incited someone to commit a crime.

Punishment

It is important to note that—irrespective of their domestic context—the more serious of the above offences attract maximum penalties of life imprisonment (mandatory in the case of murder when the perpetrator is now likely to serve some 16 years behind bars or, since 1998, following a second conviction for a serious violent or sexual offence) of 14 years imprisonment. In other words, however rapidly matters have escalated, or whatever the seething tensions, serious violent offences committed in a domestic context should result in long periods of incarceration.

The normal test of a correct sentence is that it must be commensurate with the seriousness of the offence or offences under consideration, i.e. with that offence and any other offences which are associated with it (Criminal Justice Act 1991, as amended). This is sometimes described as 'proportionality' in sentencing. However, when sentencing for violent or sexual offences courts can, if appropriate, depart from proportionality. They have, provided that they remain within the maximum sentence for a given offence, the option of imposing a heavier and longer sentence than they would have done for a violent or sexual offence if such a sentence is necessary to protect the public from serious harm from the offender.[7]

The *Magistrates' Association Sentencing Guidelines* include in their list of aggravating factors for the offence of assault occasioning actual bodily harm 'deliberate kicking or biting', 'extensive injuries', 'victim particularly vulnerable', 'premeditated' and 'weapon' all of which might be present in a domestic situation. Mitigating factors relating to the offence include 'provocation', 'impulsive' and 'single blow'. It is by weighing such factors that the court comes to its decision on seriousness and thus the correct sentence. Nothing in the guidelines specifically mentions the domestic situation indicating that this is at best a neutral factor, which cannot be put forward as an excuse or to lessen the seriousness of what has occurred. However, depending upon all the facts it may be relevant that a domestic violence perpetrator has expressed genuine remorse and co-operated with the police and is trying to make amends. This may be an indicator of whether a community sentence (perhaps a probation order with a condition attached that the perpetrator attend an intensive course or programme: *Chapter 8*) is or is not an appropriate option for consideration, a possible indicator that the offender is prepared to accept responsibility and come to terms with his behaviour. This said, if an assault is sufficiently serious 'coming to terms' may have to occur in a custodial setting.

Harassment

Two criminal offences which are likely to be of increasing significance in relation to domestic violence are those provided for in sections 2 and 4 Protection From Harassment Act 1997 (see *Chapter 7*). On conviction of either of these offence, the court can make a 'restraining order' which is in the nature of an injunction prohibiting further harassment; it is also important to note the 'cross-over' provisions as between the criminal and civil jurisdiction contained in the 1997 Act. The indications are that the provisions of this Act are being well used.

Some further considerations

In 1999, the government announced that it was considering the creation of a special statutory offence where someone is raped by an acquaintance (the so-called 'date rape') and which it might be easier to convince juries about (they, seemingly, being reluctant to find against a defendant

---

[7]   See, generally, *The Sentence of the Court*, Watkins *et al*, Waterside Press, 1999

whom the victim knew on the often critical issue of consent). Naturally, such an offence would not be without significance in the domestic context, although many people would argue against a perceived downgrading of seriousness. In any event, no details have been forthcoming. Rape remains an offence even though perpetrator and victim are married or in some regular relationship. In one Crown Court case in 1999 the accused was found guilty where the woman concerned was described as 'an especially vulnerable individual' who had become averse to sexual intercourse where the accused had intercourse with her whilst she was asleep—and even though they were in a permanent, intimate relationship.

Sex offender notifications
By virtue of the Sex Offenders Act 1997, requirements are imposed on certain sex offenders to notify the police of their name (or names), their address and any changes to these details in order to ensure that the information about sex offenders on the police national computer (PNC) is up-to-date. Notification periods start from the date of conviction and the police are informed, on conviction, that an offender is subject to such a requirement—thus allowing for rapid up-dating.

The duration of the notification depends upon the length of the sentence. A written notice of the requirement to register with the police is normally given to the defendant before he leaves court.

Sex offender orders
Quite distinct, a new sex offender order was created by the Crime and Disorder Act 1998. The police can apply for such an order against any sex offender whose present behaviour in the community gives them reasonable cause for concern and where they consider that an order is needed to protect the public from serious harm.

Magistrates' courts act under their civil jurisdiction.[8] The order requires the offender to register under the Sex Offenders Act 1997 whilst the order is in effect, and the minimum duration of the order is five years. Appeal lies to the Crown Court.

Breach of a sex offender order without reasonable excuse results in a criminal offence which, in the case of an adult, is triable either way with a maximum penalty on summary conviction of imprisonment for up to six months, or a fine not exceeding the statutory maximum or both. On conviction on indictment, the maximum term of imprisonment is five years. A fine can be imposed instead of or in addition to imprisonment. This provision was implemented in December 1998.

---

[8] When the Human Rights Act 1998 takes effect (October 2000) courts may need to treat such matters as 'criminal', at least apply the criminal standard of proof.

Bail and bail conditions

Following arrest in criminal proceedings and while the case is pending an accused person may be remanded in custody or granted bail in accordance with the Bail Act 1976. Grounds for remands in custody include the fact that the accused may repeat the offence (or commit other offences) or interfere with witnesses if not detained (normally meaning in prison for people aged 21 or over; a remand centre or young offender institution if aged 17 to 20 inclusive). If released on bail, conditions can be attached by the court or police[8] to prevent similar kinds of behaviour, e.g. to live at a particular address, keep away from certain individuals or geographical areas. The accused can be re-arrested if these conditions are breached, the likelihood being that he will face a remand in custody.

Modernising criminal law and procedure

As noted earlier in this chapter, there is no separate offence of domestic violence. Indeed, the law of assault is itself long overdue for reform, most offenders being charged under the Offences Against the Person Act 1861. In 1998 the Home Office issued a consultation paper on reform of the 1861 Act which outlined proposals about how the law concerning non-fatal offences against the person might be updated.[9] However, the proposals contain nothing specific in relation to domestic violence. As *Living Without Fear* puts matters:

> The proposals aim to modernise, improve, clarify and rationalise existing law. A new set of offences have been drafted to replace the existing offences of grievous and actual bodily harm and assault. The new offences proposed are: intentionally causing serious injury; recklessly causing serious injury; intentionally or recklessly causing injury and assault.[10]

In other words, the proposals are concerned largely with a redefinition of the mental state required (or *mens rea*) for assault rather than the particular context in which violence might occur. Separate proposals exist for the modernisation of sexual offences and to protect vulnerable witnesses.[11] The latter are contained in the Youth Justice and Criminal Evidence Bill which proposes a range of special measures, including the use of screens in court so that witnesses cannot be seen, the giving of evidence by television link, excluding people from the courtroom so that evidence is given in a private setting, allowing evidence-in-chief (the witnesses evidence at the behest of prosecution or defence and before he

---

[8] The police cannot impose a condition to reside at a bail hostel, only the court.

[9] *Violence: Reforming the Offences Against the Person Act 1861*. See also the *Law Commission Report Offences Against the Person and General Principles*.

[10] *Living Without Fear*, p.46

[11] *Ibid*, p.12

or she is cross-examined by the other party) to be given by way of a video-recorded interview, and allowing as evidence pre-recorded video cross-examination. These are bold suggestions which challenge the traditional view that the best evidence is that given in person in court from the witness-box and that hearsay or a previous statement (the recording) is not admissible. In fact, with a vulnerable witness the better evidence may come in more relaxed surroundings, while accused people may too often have used the prospect of an ordeal in court and the prospect of cross-examination to defeat justice.

PUBLIC AND PRIVATE PROSECUTIONS

It remains the case that criminal proceedings can be started by either the authorities or an individual victim.

The role of the police

Historically, there were often reservations by police about intervening in what were termed 'domestics' and maybe a tendency to play down charges. This appears to have stemmed from the idea that once an incident was over the police were just as likely to find themselves cast as the villains, with the parties united against them. This attitude has changed somewhat in recent years with police and prosecutors more prepared to domestic violence at its proper level of priority—and with courts determined to treat cases equally seriously. There remain problems of proof and evidence in some cases, and of the volatility of a given relationship in terms of seeing proceedings to a satisfactory conclusion. Nonetheless, as indicated in *Chapter 1,* there is a need to debunk the myth that women will always withdraw charges. The more serious the offence the more unlikely that anyone in the criminal justice decision-making chain might act in a way which might be viewed as condoning violence. *Living Without Fear* urges a pro-arrest policy:

> A woman's first formal contact in seeking justice will be the police. The effectiveness of the police response at that point is crucial in bringing the perpetrator to justice and preventing further violence. One of the most significant changes in police attitudes has been towards a "pro-arrest" approach as an effective means of reducing repeat victimisation. This reflects the fact that women rarely contact the police until they reach desperation. "Pro-arrest" means that where there is sufficient evidence of an offence and the police have power to make an arrest, the suspect is arrested.[12]

Other parts of that document refer to a revised circular to police on domestic violence and to the idea of 'zero tolerance' albeit there are

---

[12] *Living Without Fear,* p.32

certain problems with such strategies unless proper discretion is maintained and exercised, and police officers act on the basis of evidence as opposed to automated responses. However, an underlying problem with less formal mechanisms for confronting violence is that they can be seen as a downgrading of seriousness and a false assessment of danger.

The Crown prosecutor

Normally, supportable allegations of assault etc. made to the police result in a reference to the Crown Prosecution Service (CPS) and thereafter—assuming that there is sufficient evidence and the interests of justice require it—a prosecution will be brought in the name of the Crown. There is a duty on the Crown prosecutor to keep each case under continuous review. The *Code for Crown Prosecutors*[14] states, *inter alia* that:

> Crown prosecutors must be fair, independent and objective. They must not let their personal views of the ethnic or national origin, sex, religious beliefs, political views or sexual preferences of the offender or victim or witness influence their decisions. They must also not be affected by improper or undue influence from any source. (Para 2.3)

There are specific responsibilities to ensure that the evidence is reliable and can be used in court (the 'sufficiency of evidence test': there must be a realistic prospect of conviction) and that prosecution is required in the public interest ('the public interest test'). There are no factors in the CPS code specifically referable to domestic violence or any individual criminal offence. However, among other things, a Crown prosecutor applying the public interest test will consider factors such as the seriousness of the allegation (especially where this might result in imprisonment), whether a weapon was used or violence threatened, whether the offence was premeditated, whether the victim was vulnerable, was put in considerable fear or suffered personal attack, damage to their property or disturbance and whether there are grounds for believing that the offence is likely to be continued or repeated as a result of a history of recurring conduct.

The CPS Inspectorate published a thematic review of cases involving domestic violence in 1998 and recommendations are being implemented:

> The review covered the CPS' role in identifying domestic violence cases, providing advice to the police, and reviewing, preparing and presenting cases at court. The involvement of the CPS in local inter-agency initiatives has helped improve responses to domestic violence. The victim may be particularly vulnerable to ongoing pressure, harassment and violence from

---

[14] The Director of Public Prosecutions (head of the CPS) intends to consult the public on a new code—which might increase prosecutions generally.

the perpetrator to withdraw evidence. The CPS is responding to this problem by working with the police to improve evidence-gathering and by providing input into police training.[15]

Another initiative, *Speaking Up For Justice*, recommends that the Crown prosecutor meets the investigating police officer for 'an early strategy meeting' so as to agree the form in which the survivor's statement should be taken and what measures might be appropriate to assist witnesses in giving evidence. Other recommendations concern the care of vulnerable witnesses when attending court to give evidence. One example of good practice cited in *Living Without Fear* is Victim Support's National Witness Service which is available in every Crown Court Centre in England and Wales and this is due for extension to all magistrates' courts by April 2000. The service arranges familiarisation visits to court prior to the trial of a case; and offers separate waiting areas and relevant advice to people attending to give evidence.

Private prosecutions: A note

Albeit nowadays uncommon, failing proper action by the authorities (or a refusal to prosecute) there is a right to bring a private prosecution. A limited number of serious offences require the consent of the attorney-general.

Taking out a private summons is a simple process. The applicant visits the local justices' clerk's office, names the offence and alleged offender, and asks for a hearing to be arranged and a summons to be issued. Any difficulty lies not with the ease with which such action can be launched but the ability thereafter of the applicant to see the proceedings through. While courts have a duty to assist in a general way, it is advisable for the would be private litigant to consider whether seeing a solicitor should be his or her first step. A solicitor will advise for or against such action on the basis of an objective professional assessment. The costs of a successful prosecution are normally recoverable from public funds (including the cost of employing a lawyer) but this presupposes that the solicitor does not require advance payment or that the applicant is not destitute. It costs nothing to take out a summons in criminal proceedings but the applicant does risk costs being awarded against him or her and in favour of the defendant if the latter is acquitted or the prosecution fails for some other reason.

The CPS can take over most serious criminal prosecutions even if started privately and continue with the case or, if prosecution is deemed

---

[15] *Living Without Fear*, p.37, which also describes the CPS role as 'central to ensuring that the justice system responds effectively to crimes of violence against women (p.36)

inappropriate or the case lacks evidence, discontinue the proceedings or ask for them to be dismissed. This occurs rarely in practice.

Attrition

One aspect of crime that government now appears determined to confront—at least in relation to domestic violence—is what is known as the attrition rate:

> Of crimes committed, only a proportion are reported; of those reported, a smaller proportion are prosecuted; of those prosecuted, a smaller proportion end in conviction. This progressive reduction between crimes committed and those which end in conviction is the process known as attrition. One of the characteristics of the crimes of violence against women is the very high attrition rate.[16]

Pro-active strategies naturally impact on the attrition rate. However, the fact that there has been a high attrition rate in the past has been used as an argument to show that deterrent sentencing policies may be misguided given the true scale of offending. Attempting to reduce the attrition rate at the same time as pursuing a comprehensive strategy of deterrence, including, e.g. such items as *Break the Chain* initiatives[17] and pro-arrest policing strategies does have a more rounded logic than the notion of tough sentencing within an enforcement void.

SURVIVORS AND COMPENSATION

Criminal conviction allows the court—in addition to or instead of any sentence—to award compensation: up to £5,000 in the magistrates' court; the Crown Court can order compensation without limit. There is no formal application by the victim (Indeed, the victim, has no status in criminal proceedings, something which has been a source of concern on the part of reform groups for many years). However, the charity Victim Support is active in providing advice and assistance to victims of crime and generally in pursuing the interests of victims and witnesses. Also, any PSR prepared for the court by a probation officer should, to comply with National Standards for PSRs, contain information about the victim including where known his or her views and attitude to the offence (a relevant sentencing consideration). In addition, the police now ask all victims to fill in a form detailing any loss suffered. This information is brought to the notice of the court by the CPS.

---

[16] *Living Without Fear*, p.31. The research quoted mainly concerns rape and sexual offences (albeit many of these in a domestic context).

[17] This work, p.28

The court must give reasons if it decides *not* to make an order for compensation where there has been loss, damage or personal injury; and give priority to compensation out of available financial resources over any financial penalty.

The following guidelines are taken from the Home Office Circular issued in August 1993.

The figures below are only a very general guide and may be increased or decreased according to the medical evidence, the victim's sex, age and any other factors which appear to the court to be relevant in the particular case. If the court does not have enough information to make a decision, then the matter should be adjourned to obtain more facts.

TYPE OF INJURY		SUGGESTED AWARD
Graze	depending on size	up to £50
Bruise	depending on size	up to £75
Black eye		£100
Cut: no permanent scarring	depending on size and whether stitched	£75-£500
Sprain	depending on loss of mobility	£100-£1,000
Loss of a non-front tooth	depending on cosmetic effect and age victim	£250-£500
Other minor injury	causing reasonable absence from work (2-3) weeks	£550-£850
Loss of a front tooth		£1,000
Facial scar	however small - resulting in permanent disfigurement	£750+
Jaw	fractured (wired)	£2,750
Nasal	undisplaced fracture of the nasal bone	£750
Nasal	displaced fracture of bone requiring manipulation	£1,000
Nasal	not causing fracture but displaced septum requiring sub-mucous resection	£1,750
Wrist	simple fracture with complete recovery in a few weeks	£1,750-£2,500
Wrist	displaced fracture - limb in plaster for some 6 weeks; full recovery 6-12 months	£2,500+
Finger	fractured little finger; assuming full recovery after a few weeks	£750
Leg or arm	simple fracture of tibia, fibula, ulna or radius full recovery in three weeks	£2,500
Laparotomy	stomach scar 6-8 inches long (resulting from exploratory operation)	£3,500

Guidelines on Compensation:
Reproduced from the Magistrates' Association *Sentencing Guidelines*, 1997

Personal injuries may need to be established by medical evidence. They include physical or mental injury, so that, e.g. an award can be made for terror or distress caused by the offence. In *Bond v Chief Constable of Kent* (1982) 4 Cr. App. R. (S.) 324 the High Court held that distress or anxiety arising directly from an offence could constitute 'personal injury' or 'damage' for compensation purposes.

More recent cases have established, e.g. that assault can be committed without using direct physical force and that grievous bodily harm includes physiological injury (*R v Burstow, The Times*, 30 July 1996); and e.g. that physiological injury from an assault can occur over the telephone (*R v Ireland, The Times*, 22 May 1996). However, mere distress would not in itself constitute an assault (although it might well constitute harassment if a course of conduct is involved: see *Chapter 7*).

Guidance on sentencing and compensation

Ultimately, day-to-day sentencing law and practice is laid down by the Court of Appeal. The Magistrates' Association *Sentencing Guidelines* (1997) include aggravating factors and mitigating factors for individual offences.[18] Similar factors are reflected in the *National Mode of Trial Guidelines* (1995) and the Court of Appeal rulings following appeals from the Crown Court. Always, the fundamental questions are, as already outlined, the seriousness of the offence and the need to protect the public from serious harm from violent or sexual offenders. The Magistrates' Association guidelines also include suggested awards of compensation. After indicating that damages are assessed under two main headings (general damages for pain and suffering and any loss of facility) and special damages (financial loss sustained as a result of the injury, e.g. loss of earnings, dental expenses etc.) the Association goes on to suggest starting points based on Home Office figures: see p.41 of this work.

Victim protection and victim support

It is important that whatever strategies are in place serve to prevent victims and *a fortiori* repeat victimisation. Beyond this, if survivors do need to give evidence they must be treated sympathetically (see p.00). The 6.3 million enhancement in the level of funding to Victim Support as part of the government's 1999 initiative has been mentioned earlier. But support goes beyond this. Thus, e.g.

> It is usually — and should be — a last resort for a woman to have to leave her own home. In these circumstances it should be recognised that she is a double victim. If a woman is experiencing violence, or the threat of violence

---

[18] For both the Magistrates' Association and Mode of Trial guidelines see *The Sentence of the Court*, footnote 6.

in her relationship she may need to leave home, either temporarily or permanently. Leaving home can be an immediate response to a crisis situation, or a more planned response to a long period of abuse or violence. Local authorities have a duty to provide assistance.[17]

Various strategies are being put in place to ensure that accommodation is fairly allocated to women who have left their homes to avoid or escape domestic violence including the revision of guidance in *Allocations and Homelessness* and other information to social landlords. The role of the women's refuge and other survivor networks is mentioned in *Chapter 3.*

Criminal injuries compensation

The Criminal Injuries Compensation Scheme is intended to compensate victims of violent crime, particularly those who are seriously injured. The minimum award is currently £1,000. Courts should consider an award of compensation to a victim whether or not the injury falls within the scope of the scheme. To prevent double compensation for the same injury, any award is reduced by the amount of any compensation which has been awarded by the court. The scope and purpose of the scheme is explained in *Living Without Fear* as follows:

> The Criminal Injuries Compensation Scheme provides payments to victims of crimes of violence. Payment is based on a tariff of awards that groups together injuries of comparable severity and allocates a financial value to them. Payment can be made to victims of rape, sexual assault and adult survivors of child abuse, and those who become pregnant or infected with sexually transmitted diseases as a result of sexual violence. Such payments help to alleviate the effects of the violence and the recovery process.

The government is currently considering the responses of women's groups to a consultation document issued in 1999 inviting comments on how the scheme might be improved 'for the benefit of victims within the parameters of the current legislation'.[18]

JUDGES IN CRIMINAL PROCEEDINGS

In the Crown Court the judge is normally a circuit judge, recorder (a part-time circuit judge) or assistant recorder. In the more serious cases the judge is of the rank of High Court judge. In all cases where there is a 'not guilty' plea the issues of fact are decided by a jury under the guidance and direction of the judge. The magistrates' court is normally

---

[17] *Living Without Fear,* p.22

[18] pp.42, 43

made up of three lay magistrates (i.e. unqualified but trained) who receive legal and judicial guidance from their justice' clerk or other professional legal adviser (court clerk). In the London courts and some others, the magistrate may be a full-time or part-time stipendiary magistrate (i.e. a professional lawyer). Stipendiaries sit alone in criminal proceedings.

The government has pointed to the need for adequate training for judges and magistrates, as well as for lawyers and other practitioners.

BINDING OVER

The ancient power of magistrates to bind over citizens '. . . to be of good behaviour and keep the peace' stems from the Justices of the Peace Act 1361. More recent provisions regulate procedure. Binding over is used to mark behaviour which might lead to a breach of the peace in the future—a method known as 'preventive justice'.

The power can be used on its own, or in connection with criminal offences, in addition to any penalty. Bind overs can be made on application (often called a 'complaint') or of the court's own volition, e.g. where someone is acquitted of an offence but there is a valid reason to predict future misconduct.

The individual concerned is required to enter into a recognisance, i.e. an acknowledgement of indebtedness to the Sovereign in the event of future misbehaviour. If he or she fails to keep the peace for a period fixed by the court (usually 12 months) the amount of the recognizance is at risk. A magistrates' court may order forfeiture (sometimes called 'estreatment'), in whole or in part.

Procedure
If a court acting of its own motion proposes to bind over someone—e.g. a recalcitrant witness, or the defendant to a criminal case in addition to any penalty—this is put to that person and he or she is asked for any comments.

Where the process is started by application, the procedure follows the normal pattern for trial before magistrates. Either the defendant admits the misconduct complained of or the applicant must establish this by evidence—as well as the need for the bind over. The defendant has the usual right of reply. A bind over can be tailored to the circumstances. The good behaviour requirement can be general or specific, e.g. '. . . and especially towards [a partner, child or both]'. A refusal to be bound over is akin to contempt of court. The individual can be imprisoned or detained, but this will cease if consent is given. There is a right of appeal to the Crown Court against a binding over order.

A court considering binding over must ensure that the defendant is present, since he or she has either to enter into the recognizance or to refuse to do so (thereby risking custody: above). As often as not (and depending on the facts) private applications to bind someone over can result in cross-applications and both parties being bound over. In the past, it has not been unusual for a partner to seek this remedy—but the use of bind overs is likely to recede as a result of the newer and what will often be the more apposite protection of the harassment provisions and the power which they give to the court to make restraining orders: *Chapter 7*.[21]

Civil Proceedings

A distinction must be drawn between the general jurisdiction of the civil courts and the specialist family jurisdiction—both of which fall under the general umbrella of the High Court and county court. So far as the family jurisdiction is concerned, *Living Without Fear* notes that since Part IV Family Law Act 1996 was introduced in October 1997

> . . . statistics collected in the first year indicate that approximately 19,000 non-molestation orders to prevent violence were made, and approximately 9,000 orders dealing with occupation of the family home.[22]

THE GENERAL CIVIL JURISDICTION

Ordinarily, a civil dispute between private individuals such as an action for negligence or nuisance is dealt with by the High Court or county court depending on the value of the claim, the nature of the subject matter, and, to an extent, the wishes of the parties. A wife, say, could seek an injunction against her husband in the county court asking that he be ordered to refrain from certain types of behaviour or activities and if he failed to comply with the order he could be arrested and ultimately gaoled for contempt. In addition, or instead, she could claim damages. It was in this way that the common law tort of harassment mentioned in *Chapter 7* came to be recognised as a specific cause of action.

---

[21] Bind overs could face the same kind of human rights challenges indicated in footnote 4, *Chapter 7*. In addition, the European Court of Human Rights has held that the power to bind a person over to be of good behaviour breaches the European Convention On Human Rights as the concept of 'good behaviour' is too vague (Joseph Hashman and Wanda Harrup, Appn. 255 94/94)

[22] *Living Without Fear*, p.43

However, for all practical purposes, there is nowadays a far greater likelihood that a woman suffering domestic violence and who wishes to use the civil courts will seek relief under the family jurisdiction (below) where enhanced and more targeted remedies exist.

An application under the general jurisdiction always has to be grounded in a recognised cause action (i.e. a tort or 'civil wrong'). The standard enforcement procedure is an application for the respondent to be dealt with for contempt of court: *Chapter 6*. Causes of action which might involve interference with personal or other private rights include, e.g. trespass to the person and nuisance.

Applications for the new *statutory* tort of harassment are also part of the general civil jurisdiction of the county court and High Court, not a matter for the family courts, below. However, they are scheduled to attract special new statutory enforcement procedures: *Chapter 7*.

The remedy given under the Protection From Harassment Act 1997 is in no way restricted to people in a given relationship and apply to all and sundry. Until the Family Law Act 1996, certain categories of people—such as same sex couples, relatives or people who had been living together but were doing so no longer—were confined to the general jurisdiction. This is no longer always the case. The modern form of non-molestation order and remedies concerning occupation of the family home (below and *Chapter 3*) are available as between people who are 'associated' with one another within the meaning of the 1996 Act.

THE SPECIAL FAMILY JURISDICTION

Under the family jurisdiction three tiers of court deal with family cases:

- *the High Court of Justice* (normally the Family Division)
  Case law is also developed by judges of the High Court which assists interpretation of the law and supplements a number of Best Practice guides to decision-making or procedures, which are adhered to by all courts in the family court hierarchy. The jurisdiction of the High Court includes power to make 'non-molestation orders' and 'occupation orders' under the Family Law Act 1996 (before the 1996 Act came into force it made equivalent forms of order). Such orders are now available generally in all three tiers of court dealing with family matters and they are subject to the uniform code described in *Chapter 3*.

- *the county court*
  Some county courts have *no* family jurisdiction. Those which do, always have jurisdiction to deal with divorce, but also fall into one of three categories:

—county courts which only have a divorce jurisdiction

—family hearing centres. These county courts can, e.g. in addition to divorce cases hear contested *private law* cases (below)

—care centres. These county courts can hear *all* family matters including *public law* cases (below).

- *the family proceedings court*
  This is the name given to the magistrates' court when members of the local magistrates' court family panel sit to hear family cases. Apart from aspects of the shared jurisdiction with the county court and High Court in matters affecting children under the Children and Young Persons Act 1969, the family proceedings court deals with some other types of domestic proceedings which, historically speaking, fell to be dealt with by magistrates and cases involving the care of children by local authorities.[23] Magistrates' family proceedings courts also have quite separate powers to make maintenance orders between spouses and orders to protect spouses from one another. Under the Family Law Act 1996 they share in the jurisdiction to make non-molestation orders and orders regulating occupation of the family home: *Chapter 3*. In many instances, the family proceedings court also has a 'first stop' role' within the network of family courts described in this section: see, in particular, under the *Allocation of cases* as between family courts in *Chapter 5*.[24]

Orders available under the family jurisdiction

The jurisdiction of all three courts includes power to make the following orders:

- **non-molestation orders** to prevent *inter alia* domestic violence, and involving, where appropriate, the addition to the order of a power of arrest: sections 42 to 45 Family Law Act 1996 (*Chapter 3*)

- **occupation orders** to keep an 'associated person' (normally a spouse or partner/cohabitee) out of the family home and also involving, where appropriate, the addition of a power of arrest: sections 33 to 41 Family Law Act 1996 (*Chapter 3*)

---

[23] Care proceedings were formerly dealt with by the juvenile court, now replaced by the youth court which has an almost exclusively criminal jurisdiction

[24] And see generally *Introduction to the Family Proceedings Court*, Elaine Laken *et al*, Waterside Press, 1977

- **care orders or supervision orders** In care proceedings under the Children and Young Persons Act 1969 family courts can make either care orders or supervision orders in respect of a child under the age of 17. All care proceedings applications commence in the magistrates' family proceedings court (above). They are often finalised in that court but can be allocated to other courts in the hierarchy (*Chapter 5*). Only designated county court 'care centres' deal with care cases and it is rare for a matter to be referred to the High Court

- **enforcement orders** i.e. orders to compel compliance with other orders which courts have made: *Chapter 5.*

In addition to its shared jurisdiction and the fact that all care proceedings commence there, the magistrates' family proceedings court also has power to make:

- **emergency protection orders** to deal with any immediate threat to a child: section 44 Children Act 1989.

For completeness, it should be reiterated that the *county court* under its general civil jurisdiction (as opposed to the *family court* operating at this tier) also has power to make:

- **civil orders under the Protection From Harassment Act 1997** i.e. injunctions under section 3 (*Chapter 7*). In certain respects the ambit of these overlaps with that of non-molestation orders under the family jurisdiction (*Chapter 3*).

Care, supervision and emergency protection orders are mentioned in the next section of this chapter, *Child Protection In Outline,* along with a number of other less common orders for the protection of children.

THE JUDGES IN THE CIVIL COURTS

The judicial arrangements in the family court are as follows:

High Court
Courts are presided over by a High Court judge or deputy High Court judge. The Family Division of the High Court is presided over by the President of that division. Rulings of the judges of the High Court form binding precedents which other courts in the hierarchy must follow. In recent times, there has been an emphasis on:

- effecting practical solutions
- avoiding conflict; and
- encouraging agreement.

Domestic violence may be one area of family law where attempts at these laudable objectives are most difficult and sometimes most precarious.

County court
Most county court family work is dealt with by a district judge, a salaried appointment involving legal qualification; but with more senior judges also involved as appropriate.

Family proceedings courts
Family proceedings courts comprise three magistrates from the magistrates' family panel. A family proceedings court must include a man and a woman unless this is impracticable.

Family panel members are lay magistrates (i.e. unpaid and not possessing legal qualifications). They are advised by a justices' clerk or other professionally qualified court legal adviser. However, a family proceedings court may comprise a stipendiary magistrate (a salaried professional lawyer) as chairman and one or two lay justices who are members of the family panel. If this is not practicable, the stipendiary magistrate may sit alone.

Family panels are made up of magistrates selected by their local bench colleagues for this work on the basis of their aptitude and personal suitability. In addition to their special duties and training for the family proceedings court, members of the panel continue to serve in the ordinary magistrates' court.[23]

SOME FEATURES OF FAMILY COURTS

The way in which family courts operate departs from the way criminal courts (and to an extent other civil courts) do. They require a different 'mind-set'. One aim is to remove conflict; to get away from legal issues wherever possible in favour of practical solutions. This approach involves, for example:

- a less adversarial approach
- an investigative role for judges or magistrates
- more relaxed rules governing evidence, procedure and practice
- liaison between the various courts in the hierarchy; and

---

[23] Special arrangements exist in London where magistrates are appointed direct to the panel and do not sit in the magistrates' court as such.

- extensive cooperation between courts and other agencies.

There is also an emphasis on keeping matters 'out of court' and resolving issues by informal methods such as mediation and conciliation (though perhaps less readily if violence is involved): see *Chapter 8*. In some situations a duty is cast on legal representatives and other practitioners to encourage reconciliation and under the new divorce procedures contained in the Family Law Act 1996 (albeit currently being kept under review) the parties will be required, at the outset, to attend an information meeting. Under a system of directions hearings, many items are dealt with before a case reaches the courtroom proper, and there are procedures for the exchange of information in advance of the hearing: *Chapter 6*. In relation to children it should be noted that family courts deal with:

- *public law* cases e.g. applications for care or supervision orders which are usually brought by local authorities; and

- *private law* cases e.g. disputes between parents concerning the upbringing of children whereby orders governing the child's residence, contact with its parents and other incidents of its life are regulated.

Whilst either type of case could involve domestic violence to a child, it is with public law cases, i.e. *where the authorities step in*, that external safeguards for children exist. Local authorities have wide powers to take such action vis-à-vis a child even where a private law application is being conducted; and there is a power in the court itself to notify the local authority that an investigation is desirable.

Appeals in family cases
There is a general right of appeal to the High Court against the making or refusal to make most types of order (including under the Children Act 1989: see below). The procedure is contained in *Practice Directions* and court rules whilst case law establishes that appellants must ensure that all documents (in typescript) are lodged with the district registry of the High Court and that the court is alerted to any urgency. The High Court has wide powers to deal with the case in any way in which the lower court could have dealt with it (but is not empowered to hear evidence except in exceptional circumstances). Appeals can thereafter progress to the House of Lords, as can appeals from first instance decisions of the High Court once there has been an appeal to the Court of Appeal.

Appeals in care proceedings are governed by principles stated by the House of Lords in *G v G* 1985 1 WLR 647. In essence, where the decision involves an exercise of discretion—i.e. the lower court preferring one view of the facts to another, or one particular view of, say, a child's best interests—the appeal court will not interfere unless it considers that the lower court was plainly wrong, erred in principle, took into account something that it should not have done, or failed to take into account something that it should have done. This same general approach applies to other situations and types of proceedings.

It must be noted that magistrates do not have power to 'stay' any order (i.e. postpone its effect) when an appeal is lodged. There is an inherent power in the High Court to grant a stay on any appeal which comes to it (*O v. Berkshire County Council* (1992) 1 FLR 489).

Family Court Business Committees

Family court business committees operate throughout England and Wales from each county court care centre. They examine the process of litigation and court procedures to ensure that cases are managed efficiently and effectively, having regard to the resources available. They are chaired by a designated family judge and membership is drawn from the courts, agencies and disciplines whose practice, procedures and policies have a direct impact on family proceedings.

Local forums

Family Court Forums came into being in 1994. The aim is for representatives of regular family court practitioners to have a flexible meeting under the following terms of reference:

- to promote discussion and encourage cooperation between all the professions, agencies and organizations involved in or concerned with family proceedings and to provide occasions for this to occur at each county court care centre

- to consider issues which arise locally in the conduct of family proceedings with particular reference to the practice of the: courts, legal profession, probation service, medical profession, health authorities, social services, education authorities; and the police (as emphasised earlier in this chapter family matters may overlap with criminal acts)

- to recommend action which can be taken locally to improve the service to the parties to family proceedings; and

- to consider whether special events, seminars, study days or conferences are required in addition to routine meetings to disseminate good practice, new arrangements and ideas, or to examine problems.

Whilst such forums are concerned with the effectiveness of family proceedings, they do not have a specific interest in domestic violence (although the topic will be of considerable interest to all concerned). This specialist interest is catered for by the more recent Domestic Violence Forums which have developed in many parts of the country and which are made up, as the Family Court Forums are, of practitioners from all sides of the justice process—but with a more delineated target.

Child Protection In Outline

For the greater part, what has been described so far in this chapter assumes that the 'domestic violence'—or conflict—is between spouses, partners or adults who are in some kind of relationship to one another as envisaged by the various pieces of legislation mentioned.

CHILD CARE AND EMERGENCY PROTECTION

We have already noted earlier in this chapter that a number of criminal offences exist which are referable to victims by virtue of particular young ages. Just like any ordinary citizen who gets 'caught up' in a domestic violence situation, children also share in and enjoy the protection of the general criminal law, which is often quite rightly invoked where there is physical, psychological or sexual abuse (often misnomers for what can be quite serious *criminal* offences). Children also enjoy general rights under the ordinary civil law, even if this is not regularly relied upon by them. The factors which militate against children 'breaking out' of a family situation involving violence or abuse have already been mentioned in *Chapter 1*. The more specific civil protection for children can be summarised as follows:

- *care orders or supervision orders*
- *emergency protection orders* to deal with any immediate threat to a child: section 44 Children Act 1989; and
- two less common orders:
  —a *child assessment order*
  —a *recovery order* in respect of a child.

In addition, the police enjoy certain emergency powers without the need to resort to a court order, below.

The Family Law Act 1996 altered the Children Act 1989 so as to give additional powers to courts dealing with applications for interim care orders or emergency protection orders: see under *Exclusion requirements*, below. Emergency protection orders can normally only be made by the magistrates' family proceedings court, and all care proceedings are commenced there. The main types of order are:

- **care order** A local authority (or the NSPCC) can apply for an order placing a child in its care. The authority will then arrange either to accommodate the child itself in a community home, or, more likely nowadays, for the child to be fostered. It is possible that a child in care may be placed back with its own natural parents, either immediately or after a period of time—and there is a positive statutory duty on local authorities to seek to return the child to its parent or guardian.

    The criteria for a care order include the fact that the child has suffered or is likely to suffer 'significant harm'—defined as 'ill-treatment or impairment of health or development'—if an order is not made. Harm includes, e.g. sexual abuse, emotional abuse and neglect. In their full form the basic criteria are:

    (a) that the child concerned is suffering, or is likely to suffer, significant harm; and
    (b) that the harm, or likelihood of harm, is attributable to: the care given to the child, or likely to be given to him if the order were not made, not being what it would be reasonable to expect a parent to give him; or the child being beyond parental control. (Section 1 Children Act 1989)

Not only must 'significant harm', or its likelihood, be established, but also that the harm is attributable to a failure of reasonable parental care (the most obvious head in relation to physical or sexual abuse, or where the child needs to be removed because of the side effects of 'warring' parents) or that the child is beyond parental control. The question of whether

... harm suffered by a child is significant turns on the child's health or development, his health or development shall be compared with that which could reasonably be expected of a similar child.

In an urgent situation it is possible to obtain an interim care order.

Additionally, a residence order (i.e. controlling where the child may reside and with whom), a contact order (i.e. setting out the terms on which a parent may engage with the child) or a prohibited steps order (preventing certain things being done in relation to the child) can be made in care proceedings and can often serve to protect a child not just from a parent but also from *any other individual.*

- **supervision order** This is an order that a child be supervised by a local authority (as opposed to being placed in its care). It is subject to the same threshold criteria as a care order and comparable procedures.

- **emergency protection order** (often called an EPO). This secures intervention to protect a child, whilst giving the parents or guardians a reasonable opportunity to challenge the basis of the intervention. The order requires any person who is in a position to do so to produce the child if so requested. It authorises the removal of the child to accommodation provided by the applicant, but only in order to safeguard the child's welfare. The applicant is under a duty to return the child home if it is safe to do so. (Section 44 Children Act 1989). The application for an EPO and the order itself are reproduced in *Appendix 1.*

Further information about the welfare of children—which is always to the fore—is contained in *Appendix II* to this work. It cannot be over-emphasised that *whenever* courts—of *whatever* tier and regardless of the nature of the proceedings—are dealing with children they must have regard to relevant welfare considerations.

Exclusion requirements

Changes in schedule 6 FLA 1996 seek to address the situation where alleged sexual or physical abuse has occurred and it appears that it would not be safe for a child to remain in the environment where the alleged abuser lives (a frequent problem). Until 1997 the child itself had to be removed—and thus faced disruption—while the alleged perpetrator might continued to live in the home. The provisions allow courts to make an 'exclusion requirement' when dealing with an interim care or emergency protection application, the requirement being that the alleged abuser leaves the home—providing there is someone else living there who is able and willing to give the child the care a reasonable parent would and that person consents to the exclusion requirement.

This is achieved by new sections in the Children Act 1989: sections 38A and 38B (interim care) and sections 44A and 44B (emergency protection). They can only be used if the court is satisfied that the criteria for an interim care order or emergency protection order are also met. The form of application for an EPO and the order itself are set out in *Appendix I* to this work.

Other child care and protection provisions

In general support of child protection legislation the following more specialised items are worthy of note:

- **child assessment orders** (CAO) The purpose of a child assessment order is to supplement the powers of social workers in organizing a compulsory assessment of a child's physical, emotional or psychological well-being. Sometimes, the requirements of an emergency protection order (above) may not be met, but nevertheless there is concern about the child's welfare. (Section 43 Children Act 1989). CAOs are quite rare in practice.

- **recovery order** (RO) Where a child subject to a care order absconds or is abducted, the local authority (or NSPCC) may apply to the family proceedings court for a recovery order. The court can grant the order if it is satisfied that there is reason to believe that the child: has been unlawfully taken away or is being unlawfully kept away from the responsible person; has run away or is staying away from the responsible person; or is missing. The order also operates as a direction to any person who is in a position to do so to produce the child on request to the authorised person. (Section 50 Children Act 1989).

- **police protection** A police constable has power to remove a child to suitable accommodation and to keep him or her there, or to take reasonable steps to ensure that a child's removal from hospital or some other place in which he or she is being lawfully accommodated is prevented. (Section 46 Children Act 1989).

LEGAL REPRESENTATION

The Law Society has established a Children Panel[26] for solicitors wishing to act for children in family courts. Although not yet compulsory, in practice in *public law* cases the legal representatives of children who are instructed by a guardian *ad litem* are always drawn from the panel. The majority of representatives for other parties will also be members. Membership is open only to solicitors in private practice. Applicants must demonstrate experience of representing children in proceedings under the Children Act 1989 or show relevant advocacy experience and that cases are managed efficiently and effectively, having regard to the resources available.

---

[26] The Law Society has announced that from April 2000 the Children Panel will be extended to cover solicitors acting for *any* party in care proceedings.

MENTAL HEALTH ACT POWERS

It is not appropriate in a general book of this kind to concentrate on domestic violence problems which are attributable to the mental health or well being of the perpetrator. However, it should be noted that both criminal and civil courts possess powers to make hospital orders and guardianship orders under which people will be admitted to hospitals or other safe environments. Similarly, the police and local authorities have powers to act in an emergency. Readers wishing to pursue these aspects should seek information in specialist works.

LEGALISTIC REMEDIES: A NOTE

It is not without reason that we entitled this chapter *Law and Justice*, for these two commodities are not necessarily the same thing, and certainly not in the domestic context. Given the range of potential remedies, it might be thought that the core protections provide fairly comprehensive cover—but as emphasised in our *Preface:*

> . . . it is doubtful whether legal remedies can ever themselves provide a complete remedy for something which, at its base, is often bound up in personal and emotional considerations, the reality of which can remain hidden despite the use of formal powers.

Lord Mackay of Clashfern once pointed out when Lord Chancellor (in the context of child cases: but the sentiments seem equally applicable to the present topic):

> This is not an area where a knowledge of the black letters of the law takes one very far . . . those concerned in proceedings need to have a special depth of knowledge of relevant matters going far beyond the law . . . In addition, they may also need to come to terms with strong personal feelings . . .

Thus, legal provisions are the mechanism by which offenders are punished or disputed rights resolved; and in an emergency in relation to violence this may—and in many cases should—mean immediate action by the police to arrest and prosecute and/or a private action in the civil courts (possibly meaning an emergency or *ex parte* action)—and again as we pointed out there is now a strong momentum in favour of legal and other formal powers being used and of ensuring that incidents are not swept under the carpet. Domestic violence requires practitioners to come to terms, among other things, with issues of risk and safety, methods of restraint and appropriate punishments, and the future protection and welfare of survivors. It also has to be recognised that once a domestic arrangement does begin to deteriorate the scope for escalation is unlimited. This said, it also has to be recognised that domestic violence, however unpalatable, demands understanding on the part of those who have to deal with it. It is a similar duality which the government appears to recognise when it intones:

> We cannot achieve [safety for women and children] without recognising some of the underlying causes . . . Often these lie deep within society and so will require action over the long term to build up mutual respect. Women need timely, effective help wherever they live. And when an offence has been committed the criminal justice system must demonstrate its fairness, effectiveness and ability to meet survivors' needs.[24]

A twofold consideration

Dealing with domestic violence thus seems to involve at least a two-fold consideration: acting swiftly to confront the perpetrator—which in some cases will mean his immediate arrest and incarceration (because none of the other mechanisms described in this book are effective or appropriate)—and ensuring the protection of a survivor or potential victim from future harm or other unlawful interference. In other words, it has to be recognised that court proceedings may not be the end of the matter. By definition, all domestic conflict involves personal relationships, a longer or shorter interpersonal history of disagreement, reconciliation and a potent mix of denials and the use of power. This may involve physical, emotional, or financial power and the often mentioned 'controlling situation'. The scenario may also be one of continuing danger.

Such features rarely evaporate just because a court rules on the matter. It takes more than this for grievances to be *resolved*. Sometimes this will occur over time (it is, however, a feature of many domestic cases that they can 'run and run': the possibility of long-term danger cannot be ignored). Yet there *are* known ways of enhancing or accelerating the prospect of a real as opposed to a merely legal solution. It is for this reason that we close this book by commenting on and providing some information about prevention strategies and informal mechanisms for countering domestic violence—whenever possible before it occurs or reoccurs—and by mentioning other extra-legal initiatives designed to confront violent behaviour in a family context: *Chapter 8.*

The Leeds experiment

We also note a number of initiatives in *Chapter 8* but it is appropriate to mention here that occurring in Leeds because it is court-based. In Leeds

---

[24]*Living Without Fear*, p.8

in 1999 the country's first dedicated domestic violence court began as a pilot experiment. The aim of this project is to enhance the effectiveness of the court system both in terms of sentencing and support for victims and witnesses. The move occurred at the suggestion of a multi-agency working group under the chairmanship of the West Yorkshire Probation Service with other representatives drawn from the local bench, justices' clerk's office, Crown Prosecution Service, local lawyers, the police and organizations working with survivors of domestic violence. It must be pointed out that this is not a tribunal with any special legal status, but an ordinary magistrates' court which has been dedicated solely to domestic violence and which, at the time of writing, sits each Monday to hear cases which are so categorised. It operates under ordinary criminal law and procedures, the chief point being that the agencies have joined together to ensure that it does so to optimum effect.

CHAPTER 3

Non-Molestation and Occupation of the Family Home

In this chapter we describe in detail two remedies governed by the Family Law Act 1996: what are known as 'non-molestation orders'; and court orders which regulate occupation of the family home. For convenience, we have prefaced the latter with further details of women's refuges although it should be recognised that such places are by no means tied to people fleeing molestation or disputes concerning existing accommodation. A refuge can act as a place of safety in relation to any aspect of domestic violence and even though there is no conflict concerning rights or other issues vis-à-vis the family home.

Reform

The Law Commission report *Domestic Violence and Occupation of the Family Home* (1992) addressed what it described as two 'distinct but inseparable problems':

* protection within the family from molestation or violence; and

* occupation of the family home when relationships break down, either temporarily or permanently.

It described the existing law in this field as 'complex, confusing and lacking in integration'. The commission made several proposals which, as revised, found their way into the Family Law Act 1996. These remedies have since attained a degree of popularity. As noted in *Chapter 2*, statistics collected in the first year of operation of the 1996 Act show that approximately 19,000 non-molestation orders to prevent domestic violence were made, and approximately 9,000 orders dealing with occupation of the family home. So far as levels of seriousness are concerned the courts attached powers of arrest to nearly 80 per cent of non-molestation orders and 75 per cent of occupation orders (see p.45).

The Family Law Act 1996

The 1996 Act deals with various aspects of family proceedings:

* *Part I* contains the *underlying principles* affecting Parts II and III

- *Part II* deals with divorce and separation. These provisions were originally expected to come into force in 1999 but implementation has been deferred and those relating to no fault divorce now seem most unlikely to become law. Certain parts of the country become pilot areas for provisions relating to 'information sessions', etc. and these pilots continue: see under *Divorce and separation,* below and, more generally, *Chapter 8*

- *Part III* concerns legal aid and mediation. It has relevance to the operation of Part IV, below. It came into force on 1 April 1997

- *Part IV* came into force on 1 October 1997. It deals with:

    — domestic violence, including orders designed to ensure 'non-molestation'; and
    — occupation of the family home

- *Part V* contains supplementary provisions.

Some understanding of Parts I, II and III above is necessary before Part IV can be appreciated—and Parts I to III are more easily understood in reverse order.

Part III Legal aid and mediation
Part III seeks to divert expenditure from costly—often bitter and protracted—litigation towards helping parties to reach a negotiated, outcome: see, generally, *Chapter 8.*

Part II Divorce and separation
It was planned that the law of divorce and separation would be totally revised. In particular, Part II provided for *no fault* divorce, abolished the decree *nisi* and the decree *absolute,* and radically altered procedures. One effect of the new law was to increase the period before parties could obtain a divorce. The impact of any such delay could lead to a greater number of applications under Part IV from people concerned about what, in effect, during the waiting period, could amount to an 'interim' form of relief. The plan was that in most cases the parties to a divorce, before starting out on legal proceedings, would need to attend an 'information meeting'. This aspect continues and in the pilot areas these meetings cover such issues as:

- what facilities exist to help parties save their marriage (counselling aimed at reconciliation)

- what the divorce procedures involve

- what facilities exist to help the parties negotiate rather than litigate their divorce if it is to proceed.

In view of the government's change of heart about divorce the future is information meetings is less than clear. However, their usefulness if operated effectively cannot be denied. Information given at a meeting may serve to narrow the issues, resolve unnecessary conflict and achieve the objective of reconciliation (although when domestic violence is involved it is always necessary to proceed with extreme caution for the reasons mentioned in *Chapter 1*). The court itself may be able to refer the parties to such meetings in appropriate circumstances.

Part I: General principles for Part II (Divorce, separation and marriage counselling) and Part III (Legal aid and mediation)
Part I of the 1996 Act requires the court and other people operating under Parts II and III to observe certain fundamental principles. Whilst it should be noted that these principles do not directly affect Part IV, it is inevitable that future case law will reflect these principles across a broad range of family matters. They can be summarised:

- *The institution of marriage should be supported*

- *Spouses should be encouraged to save their marriage.* As already intimated in relation to Part III (mediation), reconciliation is to be encouraged—and spouses should take all practical steps to save their marriage, and to seek help through counselling or other avenues.

- *Breakdown of marriage.* On irretrievable breakdown, courts and all people involved should aim for minimum distress, good and continuing relationships and to avoid unreasonable costs.

- *Domestic violence.* The court and all concerned must work towards removing or diminishing the risk of violence.

Non-Molestation Orders

Within Part IV Family Law Act 1996, section 42 deals with the power to make non-molestation orders. The relevant provisions came into force in October 1997. A non-molestation order prohibits the respondent from molesting a named individual who is associated with him or her or from molesting a relevant child. The meaning of 'associated' is dealt with later in this section.

Jurisdiction

The Lord Chancellor has made an allocation order (the Family Law Act 1996 (Part IV) (Allocation of Proceedings) Order 1997: reproduced at the end of *Chapter 5*) which generally allows applications to start in any of the courts in the family court hierarchy. The Legal Aid Board will generally allow either the county court or the family proceedings court to be used and the fees that practitioners may then claim are the same in both courts. There is also a proviso in relation to family proceedings courts. Section 59 of the 1996 Act states that a magistrates' court is *not* competent to entertain any application or make any order involving

> any disputed question as to a party's entitlement to occupy any property by virtue of beneficial estate or interest or contract or by virtue of any enactment giving him the right to remain in occupation unless it is unnecessary to determine the question in order to deal with the application or make the order.

Prior to the 1996 Act, family proceedings courts had limited powers under the Domestic Proceedings and Magistrates' Courts Act 1978 to deal with applications for orders protecting spouses who were victims of domestic violence, but only in circumstances where there was the use or threat of violence—and any resulting orders only prohibited these specific forms of misbehaviour. The county court and the High Court could make orders concerning molestation (a far wider concept) under the Domestic Violence and Matrimonial Proceedings Act 1976 and could also provide remedies for cohabitees.

Meaning of 'molestation'

There is no statutory definition of 'molestation'. One dictionary definition is 'to disturb or annoy by malevolent interference or to accost or attack'. An extract from the Law Commission Report, *Family Law, Domestic Violence and Occupation of Family Home* (1994) is instructive:

> Molestation is an umbrella term which covers a wide range of behaviour. It includes any form of serious pestering or harassment . . . Any conduct which could properly be regarded as such a degree of harassment as to call for the intervention of the court . . . The degree of severity depends less upon its intrinsic nature than upon it being part of a pattern and upon its effect on the victim.

There is a good deal of case law on the meaning of molestation under the jurisdiction that the county court and High Court exercised prior to the 1996 Act. However, the statutory provisions governing their jurisdiction were repealed when Part IV of the 1996 Act came into force. It still remains to be seen exactly how the former case law on molestation will be applied, particularly as the remedy can now be considered for a wider range of people than before.

In the Family Proccedings Court at Roddenbury

Applicant Maggie Straight

Respondent Sly Pendry

                                            Case number: EG/1000/99/0

Order Family Law Act 1996

1. The respondent Sly Pendry is forbidden:
   (a) to use or threaten violence against Maggie Straight
   (b) to intimidate, harass or pester the applicant

2. The respondent is excluded from 1 Courthouse Road, Roddenbury and from going within a 500 yards radius of this dwelling-house.

3. We attach a power of arrest as there has been violence and threats of violence in the future. The power of arrest is for the duration of the order.

4. The order shall last until 28 February 2000.

Justices of the peace/clerk of the court
Dated 31 August 1999

Extract from a combined Non-molestation and Occupation Order (it is unusual in practice for such orders to be issued separately) together with a Penal Notice set out below. Details of the power of arrest—which must be set out in a further, separate notice (see p.114)—appear at p.72.

Notice A: Order includes non-molestation order—penal notice mandatory.

Important Notice to the Respondent: Sly Pendry

This order gives you instructions which you must follow. You should read it carefully. If you do not understand anything in this order ytou should go to a solicitor, Legal Advice Centre or Citizens Advice Bureau. You have a right to ask the court to change or cancel the order but you must obey it unless the court does change or cancel it.

You must obey the instructions contained in this order. If you do not, you will be guilty of contempt of court, and you may be sent to prison.

Criteria for a non-molestation order

The court must have regard to all the circumstances including the need to secure the health, safety and well being of:

- the applicant; or

- the person for whose benefit the order will be made; and

- any relevant child.

Duration of orders

A non–molestation order can be for a fixed period or until further order—but if made in other family proceedings (i.e. not proceedings exclusively to deal with non-molestation) the order will cease if that more general application is withdrawn or dismissed. The practice of the courts has been to regard non-molestation orders simply as *temporary* measures.

Who can apply?

Whenever dealing with any family proceedings (as defined in the 1996 Act) the court can make a non-molestation order *of its own motion*. If, e.g. an application is made under section 8 Children Act 1989 for a residence or contact order in respect of a child it is open to the court, if it thinks it necessary, to make such an order, even though nobody has applied for one. The following people can *apply* for a non-molestation order:

- associated persons (below)

- authorised third parties (if/when these come into being: below); or

- children under 16 years of age, when the application should be made to the High Court. (Allocation Order, Article 4.2)

Third parties

The Lord Chancellor is empowered to authorise third parties to bring proceedings on behalf of an associated person. An obvious potential third party would be the police. Parliament considered that some victims were fearful of court proceedings, and it might serve their interests if the police made the application. Traditionally police forces have been reluctant to become embroiled in *civil matters* (i.e. essentially private disputes between individuals)—but the whole emphasis of government policy is now in the opposite direction so far as domestic violence is concerned. As indicated in *Chapter 2, criminal* proceedings are not barred where violence or criminal threats are involved, especially where the matter is of such seriousness that events cannot be disregarded by prosecutors.

Meaning of 'associated person'
Prior to the 1996 Act, only spouses could apply, and in the county court and High Court 'cohabitants' in addition. The definition of 'associated person' is far wider—and is also relevant when considering applications for certain categories of occupation order (below). It is contained in s.62 of the 1996 Act and includes people who:

- are or have been married to each other

- are cohabitants or former cohabitants (further details concerning cohabitants can be found later in this chapter within the section dealing with *Occupation of the Family Home*)

- live, or have lived, in the same household other than by reason of one of them being the other's employee, a tenant, lodger or boarder. An example might be students or other people who share a house or flat rented to them by a third party.

- are relatives. The statutory list of relatives is wide-ranging and includes: father, mother, step-father, step-mother, son, daughter, step-son, step-daughter, grandmother, grandfather, grandson, brother, sister, uncle, aunt, niece, nephew.

- have agreed to marry one another. Proof of whether or not people are engaged to be married can be provided in various ways set out in the Act. Where an agreement to marry is terminated, no application can be made for a non-molestation order after three years from the date of that termination. This bar is also applicable to applications for occupation orders.

- in relation to a relevant child, are either a parent or have parental responsibility

- in relation to a relevant child who has been freed for adoption, are the natural or adoptive parents of the adopted child, the natural grandparents of the adopted child, or any person with whom the child has at any time been placed for adoption; and

- parties to existing family proceedings (other than those involving domestic violence or other applications under Part IV of the 1989 Act).

Variation and discharge

A non-molestation order can be varied or discharged by the court on application by the respondent or the person who originally applied for it. If the court made the order of its own motion, the court itself can also discharge or vary it, in this case without an application.

Content of a non-molestation order

The court may make an order prohibiting specific types of molestation or molestation generally. But the order must be sufficiently defined so that:

- the respondent can know what acts, etc. are prohibited; and

- enforcement is straightforward (see further in *Chapter 6*).

'Without notice'[1] applications

In relation to both non-molestation orders and occupation orders (below), notice must normally be given to the other party or parties and the hearing takes place with all concerned present. In exceptional circumstances an application can be made without notice, i.e. where the court hears only from one party, the individual who is applying for the order. The court must have regard to all the circumstances, including any risk of significant harm to the applicant or relevant child if the order is not made immediately, and whether or not it is likely that the applicant will be deterred or prevented from pursuing the application if an order is not made forthwith.

The court can also make an order without notice when there is reason to believe that the respondent is aware of the proceedings but is deliberately evading service. If a 'without notice' order *is* granted the court must allow representations by the party against whom it is made and who was not in attendance—as soon as this is just and convenient. See Further in *Chapters 5* and *6*.

Appeal

Appeals against decisions in relation to non-molestation orders are made to the High Court.

Non-molestation proceedings versus anti-harassment measures

For a note of some of the 'pros and cons' of taking the non-molestation route as opposed to the protection from harassment route, see *Chapter 7*.

---

[1] Seemingly it is nowadays more correct to you the term 'without notice' rather than old term *ex parte* in this context.

Women's Refuges

It is a typical feature of domestic violence that a woman may be fleeing molestation (or worse) and is experiencing problems in relation to the family home. As noted in *Chapter 1*, recent years have seen a rapid expansion in aid and support networks for survivors of domestic violence generally and in relation to refuges where they can find temporary respite in particular. The 1994 'Key Research Findings' assembled by Robin Holder and Peta Sissons[2] record, e.g. that within the women's aid network:

- 14,000 women and 21,000 children were currently living in refuges in England (WAFE, 1993)

- 36,480 women took up a refuge place in 1991/92 (WAFE, 1993)

- 5,700 women sought refuge space from London Women's Aid per year even though there were then only just over 600 bed spaces (LWA, 79/90)

- 73,869 was the estimated net demand for refuge places per year requiring about 8,200 bed spaces (LHU, 1993).

Holder and Sissons also pointed to a study from 1978 to 1980 of women in refuges by the Women's Aid Federation (Binney *et al*, 1981) which found, among other things, that:

- seven years was the average length of time a woman suffered domestic abuse (ranging from a few months to 30 to 40 years) before leaving the abuser for good

- five agencies were on average contacted by women in an effort to gain help. The two agencies most able to meet women's needs for protection and accommodation—the police and the housing department—were regarded as the least useful.

- 59 per cent of women returned home because of lack of suitable alternative accommodation

- 91 per cent of women wanted to be rehoused permanently away from their abusive partner

---

[2] *Awareness in Practice:* see p.13 of this work for details of that publication.

- 43 per cent of applicants to local authorities were not treated as homeless.

And in relation to health, welfare, housing and social services:

- a significant proportion of women sought medical help for injury, chronic illness and pain as a result of domestic violence

- 80 per cent sought medical help at least once, and 40 per cent on a minimum of five separate occasions (Dobash, 1984)

- one third of social work cases involved domestic violence (Maynard, 1985).

It is relevant in this regard that one of the government's aims as set out in *Living Without Fear* is to ensure a sympathetic response by housing departments to applications by women made homeless by domestic violence and strategies are being put in place to ensure that accommodation is fairly allocated to women who have left their homes to avoid or escape domestic violence. However, this begs the question of whether they ought to have 'been made to leave' their homes whether by a partner or as a result of any action by a social landlord—what has been described as 'double victimisation':

> It is usually—and should be—a last resort for a woman to have to leave her own home. In these circumstances we should recognise that she is a double victim. If a woman is experiencing violence, or the threat of violence in her relationship she may need to leave home, either temporarily or permanently. Leaving home can be an immediate response to a crisis situation, or a more planned response to a long period of abuse or violence. Local authorities have a responsibility to provide assistance.[3]

The government is adding a range of initiatives, including, through the Department of the Environment, Transport and the Regions, general advice to social landlords and a revised version of *Allocations and Homelessness* which incorporates a code of guidance, relevant aspects of which include rules or exhortations that local housing authorities should:

---

[3] *Living Without Fear,* p.22. The government's pledges of 'additions' to housing and emergency accommodation resources are set out at p.23 of that document. The Department of the Environment, Transport and the Regions has published *Relationship Breakdown: A Guide for Social Landlords* which provides landlords with information about aspects of housing and family law affecting the rights and responsibilities of landlords and tenants, including issues raised where domestic violence is the reason for relationship breakdown.

- consider waiving any residential requirement they have for entry to the housing registers to allow access to people from another district if they are fleeing domestic violence;

- consider invoking emergency procedures to make a speedy allocation where necessary;

- treat people who have suffered domestic violence as having 'reasonable preference' because they have a welfare need for settled accommodation;

- give reasonable preference to women occupying refuges on the ground that they are in accommodation that is insecure;

- treat people fleeing domestic violence as homeless, because it is not reasonable for them to return to the accommodation they have left and they should not be referred back to the authority from whose area they have fled;

- when appropriate treat people recovering from the effects of violence as vulnerable and therefore as having a priority need for accommodation (i.e. authorities *may* do this).

In relation to refuges specifically, the government notes that

> Some women fleeing violence need safe accommodation and services that give them physical protection, confidentiality, support and advice to help them deal with the situation. It was to meet this combination of needs that the refuge movement, initiated and still run largely by the voluntary sector, was established. It has grown from the first refuge established in 1871 to a well-established network of over 400 refuges in England and Wales . . . Women can use refuge accommodation as a breathing space while they plan what to do next. Some will decide to pursue legal remedies such as injunctions and/or exclusion orders so that they can return home. Those unable or unwilling to return home for fear of further violence will need alternative accommodation.[4]

The government also instances examples of good practice, including the work of the nationwide umbrella charity Women's Aid which has a membership of 250 local domestic violence projects and now provides refuge for 53,000 women and children each year, and outreach support and help to a further 150,000 women survivors (in addition to other associated work detailed in *Living Without Fear*). The government also instances Refuge, the national charity and provider of help and support

---

[4] *Living Without Fear*, p.23

to women and children escaping domestic violence which now provides a safe place for up to 1,200 women and children each year as well as other key services.[5]

Occupation of the Family Home

Under the Family Law Act 1996, courts can regulate the occupation of 'the family home'. This jurisdiction is shared between the High Court, county court and family proceedings court in most instances. Orders affecting occupation of the family home are in practice referred to under Categories 1 to 5 which are described in the remainder of this chapter. It is essential to know which category an applicant falls into because this affects:

- the criteria which the court must consider and adhere to
- the content of the order; and
- the duration of the order.

If someone applies under the wrong category, the court itself can determine to treat the application as if made within the correct category.

CATEGORY 1: APPLICANT ENTITLED TO OCCUPY THE RELEVANT PROPERTY (S.33 FLA 1996)

Anyone with rights to occupy is entitled to apply under *Category 1* provided that the home was intended to be the parties' common home. The right to occupy may be either by virtue of

- the general law; or

- matrimonial home rights (see next page).

---

[5] *Living Without Fear*, p.24. The contact details are as follows: Women's Aid Federation of England, PO Box 391, Bristol BS99 7WS. Tel 0117 944 4411. E-mail:wafe@wafe.co.uk; Refuge, 2-8 Maltravers Street, London WC2R 3EE. Tel 0171 395 7700. Other examples of good practice are cited, including the Black Association of Women Step Out Ltd (BAWSO), Beverley Lewis House (a temporary refuge for women with learning difficulties) and a number of crisis centres for those suffering sexual interference of various kinds.

Application may be made against anyone with whom the applicant is associated. The definition of 'associated' is the same as in relation to *Non-molestation Orders*: see page 65.

Rights to occupy under the general law
These arise by virtue of a current and lawfully enforceable tenancy or from joint ownership of the property concerned.

Matrimonial home rights
A *spouse* who has no property rights in connection with the family home has a right by law not to be evicted from the home without the leave of the court, or if he or she has been unlawfully evicted to apply to the court for leave to reoccupy. These are usually referred to as 'matrimonial home rights'.

Types of order under Category 1
Two types of orders can be made in respect of *Category 1* applicants:

• *a declaratory order* This simply declares that the applicant has matrimonial home rights in a house, flat etc. in respect of which there may be a dispute, e.g. as to whether it is in fact a family home or, say, an investment property. Matrimonial home rights (above) normally cease on divorce (and do not pass to anyone with the estate or otherwise upon death). Under this category, an application could be made for the right not to be evicted without the leave the court to be extended beyond divorce. The court has a wide discretion, i.e. to 'exercise its powers . . . in any case where it considers that in all the circumstances it is just and reasonable'. The power to make a declaratory order is, by its very nature, only applicable to spouses.

• *a regulatory order* This power exists where either party is associated with the other (see p.65) and this could include, e.g. the situation where a brother and sister have been living in the same house provided it was their joint family home. A regulatory order can contain provision for one of the parties to leave the property, or it could affect the nature of occupation (e.g. a requirement for one party to live in one part of the property and the other party to live in another part). In deciding whether a regulatory order is appropriate the court must have regard to all the circumstances and in particular to the:

—housing needs and resources of the parties and any children
—financial resources of the parties

—likely effect of an order (or lack of one) on the health, safety and well being of the parties or any relevant child; and

—conduct of the parties in relation to each other and otherwise.

In the Family Proceedings Court **Power of Arrest** Family Law Act 1996		Case number EG/1000/99/0
	Maggie Straight Sly Pendry	**Applicant** *Ref* **Respondent** *Ref*
The Court orders that (here set out those provisions of the order to which this power of arrest is attached and no others)	a power of arrest applies to the following paragraph(s) of an order made under this Act on the See attached order paragraphs 1-3	
Power of Arrest	The court is satisfied that the respondent has used or threatened violence against the [applicant] Maggie Straight [and there is a risk of significant harm to the applicant[[and] [or] the above child[ren]] attributable to the conduct of the respondent if the power of arrest is not attached immediately.] A power of arrest is attached to the order whereby any constable may (under the power given by section 47(6) of the Family Law Act 1996) arrest without warrant the respondent if the constable has any reasonable cause for suspecting that the respondent may be in breach of any provision to which the power of arrest is attached.	
This Power of Arrest expires on	29 February 2000	
Note to the Arresting Officer	Where the respondent is arrested under the power given by section 47 of the Family Law Act 1996, this section requires that: the respondent must be brought before the court within 24 hours of the time of his arrest and if the matter is not then disposed of forthwith, the court may remand the respondent. Nothing in section 47 authorises the detention of the respondent after the expiry of the period of 24 hours beginning at the time of his arrest, unless remanded by the court. The period of 24 hours shall not include Christmas Day, Good Friday or a Sunday.	
Ordered by	[Mr] [Mrs] Justice [His] [Her] Honour Judge [Deputy] District Judge [of the Family Division] Justice[s] of the Peace [Assistant] Recorder on 31 August 1999	
FL406 Power of Arrest		

Power of arrest—Combined Non-molestation and Occupation Order: see p.63 and for details of enforcement *Chapter 6.*

The balance of harm test

The above factors are also subject to a balance of harm test. Under section 33(7) Family Law Act 1996 this test is as follows:

> If it appears to the court that the applicant or any relevant child is likely to suffer significant harm attributable to conduct of the respondent if an order under this section containing one or more of the provisions mentioned in sub-section (3) is not made, the court shall make the order unless it appears to it that—
>
> (a) the respondent or any relevant child is likely to suffer significant harm if the order is made; and
>
> (b) the harm likely to be suffered by the respondent or child in that event is as great as, or greater than, the harm attributable to the conduct of the respondent which is likely to be suffered by the applicant or child if the order is not made.

The reasoning behind the balance of harm test and the effect it should have in practice was predicted by the Law Commission:

> In cases where the question of significant harm does not arise, the court would have power to make an order taking into account . . . (relevant) factors . . . but, in cases where there is a likelihood of significant harm this power becomes a duty and the court must make the order after balancing the degree of harm likely to be suffered by both parties and any children concerned. This approach would still work in cases of cross application where the court would firstly consider who would suffer the greatest risk of harm if the order were not made. In the event of the balance of harm being equal, the court would retain power to make an order, but would have no duty to do so, and would still be able to reach the right result. Harm has a narrower meaning than hardship. It is defined as 'ill-treatment or impairment of physical or mental health'. In relation to children the term will attract the definition used in section 31 Children Act 1989.[6] It is likely that a respondent threatened with ouster on account of his violence would be able to establish a degree of hardship, but he is unlikely to suffer significant harm whereas his wife and children who are being subject to his violence or abuse may very easily suffer harm if he remains in the house. In this way the court will be treating violence or other forms of abuse as deserving immediate relief, and will be directed to make an order where significant harm exists.

How long can a Category 1 order last?

Declaratory orders are not affected by time considerations. *Regulatory* orders may—with continuing effect—be for:

---

[6] See, generally, for the welfare of children *Appendix II* to this work.

- a fixed period
- until the occurrence of a specified event; or
- until further order.

Regulatory orders cannot be for an indeterminate period. The former 'ouster' order in the county court (the nearest comparable remedy) was generally treated as a *temporary* measure, to give the parties time to resolve their dispute permanently. The law on occupation orders is likely to develop in the same way.

CATEGORY 2: WHERE THE APPLICANT IS A FORMER SPOUSE WITH NO EXISTING RIGHT TO OCCUPY AND THE RESPONDENT IS THE OTHER FORMER SPOUSE WITH A LEGAL RIGHT TO OCCUPY (S.35 FLA 1996)

When a spouse has matrimonial home rights he or she can apply under *Category 1* above. On divorce, such rights come to an end unless extended by a court following an application under that category as explained above. Where this has not happened, a former spouse can apply for an order under *Category 2*.

Types of order under Category 2

Occupation orders under this category *must* contain a *declaratory* provision giving similar rights to the former spouse as he or she would have had if the marriage had not come to an end and the spouse had matrimonial home rights. In other words, if the court considers that an order should be made, the applicant who is the former spouse should, at the very least, be put into the same position as if the marriage had continued.

In addition, the court has *a discretion* to make provision *regulating* occupation of the property and similar to that described in relation to *Category 1* (e.g. requiring the respondent to leave the property or excluding him or her from a specified part of it).

Extra criteria for Category 2 orders

In deciding whether to grant an occupation order, the court will consider similar factors to those mentioned in relation to *Category 1*. In addition, three factors specific to ex-spouses not entitled to occupy the property must be considered. These are:

- the length of time since the parties ceased to live together

- the length of time since the marriage was dissolved or annulled; and

- the existence of certain pending proceedings between the parties.

In some instances it will be more difficult for ex-spouses to obtain an occupation order. If a significant time has elapsed since the parties ceased to live together or the marriage ended, this will tend to tell against making an order. Similarly, if other proceedings are pending in connection with the former matrimonial home, a court dealing separately with a *Category 2* application might well consider that an occupation order would not be appropriate.

The balance of harm test

The balance of harm test described in relation to *Category 1*, if.relevant, applies to create a presumption that the court will make an order containing one or more of the regulatory provisions.

How long can a Category 2 order last?

One difference between *Category 1* and *Category 2* orders is that the latter variety cannot continue after the death of either party, and must be for a maximum of six months—although the six months period can be renewed on one or more occasions for further specified periods not exceeding six months.

CATEGORY 3: WHERE THE APPLICANT IS A COHABITANT/EX-COHABITANT WITHOUT AN EXISTING RIGHT TO OCCUPY (S.36 FLA 1996)

In this situation the other party will be the corresponding cohabitant or ex-cohabitant who has a right to occupy.

Definition of 'cohabitant'

Section 62(1) Family Law Act 1996 defines cohabitants as follows:

(a) 'cohabitants' are a man and a woman who, although not married to each other, are living together as husband and wife; and

(b) 'former cohabitants' is to be read accordingly, but does not include cohabitants who have subsequently married each other.

It should be noted that couples must have lived together 'as husband and wife', so that same sex couples are excluded as the law stands and thus only eligible to make applications if they fulfill the criteria under *Category 1*. Living together as husband and wife will normally involve a shared life and living arrangements and a sexual element. Apart from the bare wording of section 62(1) above, existing case law will probably be applicable to disputes about whether someone is or is not a cohabitant—although the question is ultimately an question of fact. The reader is referred to specialist works.

What can a Category 3 order contain?
As with a *Category 2* order, certain *declaratory* provisions must be inserted which are similar to those a spouse would obtain who had matrimonial home rights. In addition, the court has a discretion to impose *regulatory* provisions similar to those under *Category 1*.

Extra criteria for a Category 3 order
Similar factors must be considered under *Category 3* as for *Categories 1* and 2, including the length of time since the partners ceased to live together and the existence of any pending proceedings for financial relief under the Children Act 1989 or pending proceedings relating to the legal or beneficial ownership of the property concerned. In addition, the court must take into account certain factors specific to cohabitants. These are:

- the nature of the parties' relationship

- whether there are or have been any children who are children of both parties of whom both parties have or have had parental responsibility; and

- the length of time during which they have lived together as husband and wife.

Although the court must consider the likelihood of a party or any child suffering significant harm attributable to contact with the respondent, these questions do not impose a duty on the court to make the order. The balance of harm test (see p.73) merely operates as a further factor to be weighed by the court within an exercise of discretion: contrast the position in relation to spouses and entitled parties, above.

How long can a Category 3 order last?
A *Category 3* order may be made *only* for a maximum period of six months and may be renewed *only* once, for a further specified period not exceeding six months.

CATEGORY 4: WHERE THE APPLICANT IS A SPOUSE OR EX-SPOUSE AND NEITHER THE APPLICANT NOR THE RESPONDENT HAS A RIGHT TO OCCUPY (S.37 FLA 1996)

A spouse or ex-spouse may make an application for an order where neither party is entitled to occupy the property. In this case the order will only operate as between the parties and not bind or affect a third party (who may, e.g. be entitled to exclusive occupation of the property). An example of such a situation could be where the parties have married but are, say, living with in-laws rather than independently in their own home.

Contents of a Category 4 order
The order will only contain *regulatory* provisions similar .to those described in relation to *Category 1* above. It is not appropriate under this head for there to be any *declaratory* provisions as none of the parties have rights of occupation of the home to which such a declaration could attach so as to be of any effect.

Extra criteria for a Category 4 order
Category 4 has a list of factors similar to those in relation to *Category 1*. The one main difference between an application under *Category 4* and one under *Category 1* is that under *Category 4* both parties must be in occupation.

Balance of harm test
The balance of harm test applies to create a presumption that the court will make an order containing one or more regulatory provisions.

How long can a Category 4 order last for?
An order under *Category 4* may be for a maximum period of six months, but can be renewed on one or more occasions for further specified periods not exceeding six months.

CATEGORY 5: WHERE THE APPLICANT IS A COHABITANT OR EX-COHABITANT AND NEITHER THE APPLICANT NOR THE RESPONDENT HAS A RIGHT TO OCCUPY (S. 38 FLA 1996)

A cohabitant or ex-cohabitant (see the explanation of this term at p.75 above) may make an application for an order where neither party is entitled to occupy the property. In this case the order will only operate as between the parties and will not, e.g. bind or affect a third party who is entitled to exclusive occupation of the property.

Contents of a Category 5 order
As with *Category 4* orders, an order under *Category 5* will only contain *regulatory* provisions similar to those described in relation to *Category 1* above. It is not appropriate under this heading for there to be any *declaratory* provisions as none of the parties have rights of occupation.

Criteria for a Category 5 order
The following basic items need to be considered in addition to all the circumstances of the case:

- the financial needs of the parties

- the financial resources of the parties

- the effect of any order or lack of one on the health, safety and well being of the parties or any relevant child; and

- the conduct of the parties.

The test relating to significant harm operates in the same way as it does in relation to a non-entitled cohabitant against an entitled cohabitant under *Category 3*. It does not impose a duty on the court to make an order.

How long can a Category 5 order last for?
A *Category 5* order can last for up to six months and is renewable, but only once for a further specified period of up to six months.

SOME GENERAL CONSIDERATIONS

Several general items are relevant to the above applications:

- *marriage and commitment* It might be thought that all people, whatever their status, should be treated in the same way by courts. However, due to political pressure an amendment occurred to the FLA 1996 (as now contained in section 41). The provision states that when dealing with an application by a cohabitant or ex-cohabitant the court 'is to have regard to the fact that they have not given each other the commitment involved in marriage'.

- *ancillary orders* When a court makes an order against an entitled respondent it may make an ancillary order imposing obligations on either party, or granting possession or use of furniture or other home contents. These highly significant obligations may relate to:

    —repair and maintenance of the home
    —discharge of outgoings (e.g. rent, mortgage)
    —payment of rent to the party who has been ousted
    —taking reasonable care of the furniture or other contents; or
    —taking reasonable steps to keep the home and contents secure.

    Any ancillary order remains effective for the period of the occupation order.

- *child applicants* A child under 16 years of age may apply for an occupation order but only with the leave of the court. Leave will only be granted if the court is satisfied that the child has sufficient understanding. Such applications must be made to the High Court.

- *power to make an order of the court's own motion* Whereas in any family proceedings a court can make a non-molestation order of its own motion, i.e. without an application from a party (see earlier in this chapter), no such inherent power exists in relation to occupation orders. A court can only make an occupation order if someone applies for one.

PROCEDURES AND ENFORCEMENT

Separate information and materials concerning procedures, *ex parte* orders, powers of arrest and enforcement of non-molestation orders and occupation orders is contained in *Chapters 5* and *6* of this work. *Chapter 5* also contains a copy of the combined application for and notes for guidance.

CHAPTER 4

Undertakings (Section 46 FLA 1996)

An important aim when dealing with personal interference is to ensure that it ceases as soon as possible, ideally straightaway. This will often require action under the civil or criminal jurisdictions described in this book, and in certain circumstances the effects can be accelerated either by the arrest of the perpetrator or by making an *ex parte* application to a civil court. In some instances the same objective may be achieved by the perpetrator, in effect, promising to behave properly towards the victim.

Under pre-Family Law Act 1996 Act procedures, the High Court and county court when dealing with applications for injunctions regularly accepted what are known as undertakings. Part IV of the 1996 Act extended this concept to the family proceedings court—so that in appropriate circumstances undertakings are now possible in all courts in the family court hierarchy.

An undertaking (see the specimen form opposite) is a promise by a party to do or to refrain from doing something. This might involve, e.g. leaving the family home and agreeing ('undertaking') not to go within a certain distance of it. It is important that an undertaking is precise and capable of enforcement.

Most obviously, an undertaking can operate as an alternative to a non-molestation or occupation order if accepted by a party to such proceedings and approved by the court. Indeed, under the 1996 Act, courts may accept an undertaking from *any* party to proceeding where it has power to make an occupation order or non-molestation order: see, generally, *Chapter 3;* and *Chapter 5* for a note about procedures.

Limits to the use of undertakings
Under Part IV of the 1996 Act, an undertaking *cannot* be accepted in situations where the court, if making an order, would have attached a power of arrest. A power of arrest must be attached to an order if violence or threatened violence has been present unless the court is satisfied that any order would provide adequate protection without the need for a power of arrest. Similarly, if an undertaking is offered in situations where violence or threats of violence have actually occurred, it cannot normally be accepted—but, e.g. where the application alleges violence, but the parties after considering legal advice ask the court to accept an undertaking and specifically not to rule on the issue of violence, many courts will, where appropriate, accept an undertaking.

In the	**Magistrates' Court**
	Case Number

This form is to be used only for an undertaking, not for an injunction.	**General Form of Undertaking** Family Law Act 1996

Applicant
Ref:
Respondent
Ref:

On the   day of

(1) Name of the person giving undertaking

(1)
(appeared in person) (was represented by) (Solicitor) (Counsel)

(2) Set out the terms of promising the undertaking

and gave an undertaking to the Court
(2)

(3) Give the date and time or event when the undertaking will expire

And to be bound by these promises until (3)

The Court explained to (1)

the meaning of his undertaking and the consequences of failing to keep his promises

(4) The court may direct that the party who gives the undertaking shall personally sign the statement overleaf

And the Court accepted his undertaking (4) (and *if so ordered* directed that

should sign the statement overleaf

(5) Set out any other directions given by the court

And the Court ordered that (5)

Ordered by   **Justice(s) of the Peace**

On

Important Notice

(6) Address of the person giving the undertaking

To (1)
Of (6)

- You may be sent to prison for contempt of court if you break the promises that you have given to the court.*

- If you do not understand anything in this document you should go to a solicitor, Legal Advice Centre or a Citizens' Advice Bureau. *(continued)*

General Form of Undertaking (Statement)

The court may direct that the party who gives the undertaking shall personally sign the statement opposite	Statement I understand the undertaking that I have given, and that if I break any of my promises to the court I may be sent to prison for contempt of court* Signed Date
To be completed by the Court	Delivered: • By posting on • By hand on • Through a solicitor on Signed: (Officer) Date:

Specimen form of undertaking

The above is the form of undertaking FL 422 (magistrates' courts) based upon and the equivalent of form N117 (county courts).

* In the case of the family proceedings court, this should be taken to mean enforcement pursuant to section 63 Magistrates' Courts Act 1980: *Chapter 5*

Effect of an undertaking
If the parties agree an undertaking the court cannot refuse to accept it other than in the situation already mentioned above in relation to violence or threats of violence. Neither can the court insist that the allegations are proved, and it cannot make some other kind of order.

Advantages of an undertaking
An undertaking is often viewed as having advantages:

- from the applicant's point of view, he or she is given similar protection to when an order is made

- from the respondent's point of view, it means that he or she does not have to admit or become legally bound by the facts; and

- from the court's point of view, it avoids the need for a contested hearing.

The only practical legal difference—though perhaps important—is that a power of arrest can only be attached to a court order, not to an undertaking. Nonetheless, if an undertaking is breached enforcement methods exist (below and *Chapter 6*); and proceedings can still be brought for any of the other remedies described in this book.[1]

The process of giving an undertaking
Undertakings in family proceedings courts are given in Form FL422 under a procedure similar to that existing in the county court before the 1996 Act. In neither the county court or family proceedings court is there any provision allowing an undertaking to be given in the absence of the person giving it. This is because of the importance of the giver understanding the order, its precise provisions and the consequences of breaching it. In practice some county court judges allow undertakings to be given 'in absence' but only where the respondent's solicitor himself or herself gives and 'undertaking' to the judge to personally explain all relevant matters to his or her client. The court is usually responsible for delivering the form of undertaking to the giver.

Enforcement of undertakings
An undertaking binds the giver from the moment it is accepted by the court and is enforceable as if it were an order of the court. The position is explained in *Chapter 6*. It is important that the court ensures that the giver of the undertaking understands the exact nature of his or her promises to the court and the possible consequences if breached.

Variation of undertakings
It is likely that an undertaking will be limited to a specified period of time. It remains open for an undertaking, while in force, to be varied by way of a subsequent undertaking on fresh terms.

---

[1] Undertakings might be viewed as at odds with proactive strategies to 'toughen up' on domestic violence *Chapter 1*, and acceptance by a court as downgrading violence, even as dangerous. This has to be balanced against the fact that a man who offers to give an undertaking could be starting to come to terms with his behaviour. As noted above, a court can (in some cases must) refuse to accept an undertaking if violence or threats are involved. Criminal proceedings are not barred in any event, then or later: see generally *Chapter 2*.

CHAPTER 5

Procedure

Procedures for obtaining the remedies outlined in this book are either of a general nature or specific to the subject matter under consideration. In some cases, they are, in effect, an integral part of the subject matter and in others can be conveniently discussed separately. The overall position is as follows:

- criminal proceedings are usually commenced by a professional prosecutor and an understanding of this process only really becomes relevant in the case of a private prosecution. We have already outlined what is involved (p.39). For a more detailed explanation of the summary justice process see *Introduction to the Magistrtates' Court*, Bryan Gibson, Waterside Press, 1999.

- similarly, the way in which proceedings are brought under the normal civil jurisdiction (meaning in the High Court or county court) is a matter of general import.

- special application and enforcement procedures apply under Part IV Family Law Act 1996 to non-molestation orders, occupation orders and undertakings: these are outlined in this and the next chapter.

- special procedures apply in care proceedings in relation to children and we have included the forms relating to emergency protection orders in *Appendix I*. For more general information about care proceedings it is better to consult specialist works such as *Introduction to the Family Proceedings Court*, Elaine Laken *et al*, Waterside Press, 1997.

- in earlier chapters it was noted that, in some cases, issues of domestic violence can occur when a court is dealing with cases under the Children Act 1989. Those proceedings are governed by the Family Proceedings Court (Children Act 1989) Rules 1991 in so far as proceedings in the family proceedings courts are concerned and Part IV of the Family Proceedings Rules 1991 (as amended) in relation to proceedings in the county court.[1]

---

[1]   Again, this happens within the broader and specialist context of child welfare. Practitioners requiring further details are referred to *Introduction to the Family Proceedings Court*, already referred to in the text.

The remainder of this chapter concentrates on the procedures for the special procedures governing applications for orders under Part IV of the Family Law Act 1996, i.e. non-molestation orders and occupation orders and the allocation of cases between courts in the family court heirarchy.

PROCEDURES IN PART IV FLA CASES

The procedural rules affecting applications under Part IV Family Law Act 1996 are contained in

- the Family Law Act 1996 (Part IV) (Allocation of Proceedings) Order 1997.

- the Family Proceedings Rules 1991 (as amended by the Family Proceedings (Amendment No. 3) Rules 1997) as far as the *county court* is concerned (described in this work as the 'FPR rules'); and

- the Family Proceedings Courts (Matrimonial Proceedings etc.) Rules 1991 (as amended by the Family Procedings Court (Matrimonial Proceedings etc.) (Amendment) Rules 1997) in respect of the *family proceedings court* (described in this work as the 'FPC rules').

The allocation order—which also deals with the transfer of cases between courts—is reproduced at the end of this chapter. Extracts from the other statutory instruments above are also reproduced at the end of the chapter together with a copy of the prescribed application form and official *Notes for Guidance.* All three measures are discussed in the text.

For the magistrates' family proceedings court the major changes wrought by the latest amendment to the rules are found in rule 3A and 12A and in the county court in rule 3. There is little difference between the procedures in the two courts, the main subtleties being to cater for the differing functions of the justices' clerk as professional adviser to (usually) lay of justices of the peace in the family proceedings court as opposed to the professional district judge in the county court.

Both sets of rules generally follow the format of the court rules under the Children Act, in particular by setting out prescribed forms for applications and giving the courts wide powers to give directions for the conduct of proceedings. The magistrates' family proceedings court has experienced the greatest change (including in relation to enforcement procedures which have been brought into line with the pre-1996 procedures operating in the county court (*Chapter 6*)). The approach we have adopted is to describe the position as it exists in the family proceedings court and to note where this differs in the county court, i.e.

whenever there are significant procedural differences between the family proceedings court and the county court this is made clear.

ALLOCATION OF CASES

As indicated above, the law governing allocation is contained in the Family Law Act 1996 (Part IV) (Allocation of Proceedings) Order 1997. The scheme is quite similar to that for private law proceedings under the Children Act 1989. Generally speaking, the applicant has the right to chose which tier of court to commence proceedings in, subject to certain statutory exceptions. There are then rules giving the courts wide powers of case management to ensure that a particular matter is heard in the appropriate court and tier. In practice, since the introduction of the FLA 1996, the majority of Part IV applications, particularly those for occupation orders tend to be heard in the county court. The allocation rules appear at the end of this chapter.

Starting the proceedings

Article 4(1) of the 1997 Order provides that proceedings may be commenced in a county court or family proceedings court except that any application by someone under the age of 18 must be made to the High Court—and the leave of the High Court is required, in any event, before a child under the age of 16 may commence proceedings (Article 4(2)). Furthermore, any application to extend, vary or discharge a non-molestation order or occupation order must be made to the court that made the original order (Article 5(1)).

JURISDICTION

County courts which have jurisdiction to deal with applications are those which are designated as either:

- divorce county courts
- family hearing centres; or
- care centres.

In connection with magistrates' courts it should be noted that only the family proceedings court can deal with applications, but that there is an exception in relation to later enforcement proceedings in respect of an order under Part IV. These fall within the ambit of s.65(2) Magistrates' Courts Act 1980 which means that they can either be classified as family proceedings and dealt with in private by family panel justices or—if not so classified—can be dealt with by any justices, whether from the family panel or not (i.e. in effect either in the family proceedings court or the ordinary magistrates' court) within the commission area. Many magistrates' courts have not classified such proceedings as family proceedings to allow ordinary adult justices sitting e.g. as a 'remand court' on a Saturday morning to deal with respondents arrested for breach of a Part IV order without having to make extra arrangements to call in justices from the family panel: for *Enforcement* generally, see *Chapter 6*.

TRANSFER OF CASES

The rules allow for transfer between courts in the family court heirarchy as appropriate.

Transfer by the family proceedings court

The family proceedings court may transfer an application under Part IV to another family proceedings court where there are family proceedings pending in that court and the transferring court considers it appropriate for both sets of proceedings to be heard together. Any such transfer is subject to obtaining the prior consent of the justices' clerk of the receiving court (Article 7). A family proceedings court may (either upon application or of its own motion) transfer proceedings under Part IV to the county court where:

- there are family proceedings pending at the county court and the family proceedings court considers that it would be appropriate for the proceedings to be heard together; or

- there is a conflict with the law of another jurisdiction; or

- there is some novel or difficult point of law; or

- some question of general or public interest arises; or

- where the proceedings in question are exceptionally complex.

(Article 8(1))

In practice, very few transfers are actually made because practitioners tend to commence proceedings in the county court to start with if any of these criteria are likely to apply.

A family proceedings court *must* transfer proceedings under Part IV to the county court where a child under the age of 18 is either a respondent to the application or wishes to become a party to the proceedings, or when any party to the proceedings suffers from a mental disorder (within the meaning of the Mental Health Act 1983) if his or her condition renders him or her incapable of managing and administering his or her property and affairs (Article 8(2)).

Transfer by the High Court and county court
Both the High Court and county court have power to transfer proceedings under Part IV to a family proceedings court if one of those courts considers that it would be appropriate for the proceedings to be heard with other proceedings pending in that family proceedings court or where, in the case of the county court, the judge considers that the criteria referred to in Article 8(1) above do not apply. This could occur either when an application has been transferred from the family proceedings court to the county court based on one or more of those criteria, or, say, where an application has actually been started in the county court. The transfer power is not used frequently but the authors are aware of situations where county courts with particular problems of delay have transferred free-standing non-molestation order applications to the family proceedings court by way of agreements reached with a family proceedings court in discussions at local Family Court Business Committees.

THE APPLICATION ITSELF

Proceedings are commenced by completing a prescribed form, the form being identical whichever court the application is made in, namely Form FL401 (rule 3(A)(1) FPC rules; rule 3.8(1) FPR rules).

This same form is used for applications for both non-molestation orders and occupation orders—of whatever type—and consists of six pages and eleven multi-part questions. Form FL401 together with the explanatory *Notes for Guidance* is reproduced at the end of *Chapter 3*.

Family proceedings court
In the family proceedings court, the application must be supported either

- by a written statement which is signed and declared to be true; or
- with the leave of the court, by oral evidence. This provision for oral evidence was made to cover those situations where there is an urgent or *ex parte* application. It should not be used as a means of circumventing the requirement for a written statement of evidence.

High Court and county court
In the High Court or county court the application must be supported by an *affidavit* (a sworn written statement) unless leave is given for oral evidence.

General requirements in either court
Unless expressly stated, the remaining procedures are common to all courts. The applicant must file sufficient copies of form FL 401 and a supporting statement or affidavit (as applicable) for these to be served on the respondent (i.e. at least two copies).

The procedure can be contrasted with private law proceedings under the Children Act where no statement can be filed without the leave of the court. The rationale for the position under the Children Act is that parties should be discouraged from making damning statements against each other before mediation can be considered.[2]

Notice of hearing
Upon receipt of the documents filed by the applicant the justices' clerk or in the county court the proper officer must fix the date, time and place for a hearing or directions appointment, endorse this on the copies of the application and return this documentation together with Form FL402 (Notice of Hearing) and Form FL415 (Statement of Service) to the applicant allowing him or her sufficient time for service of these documents on the respondent.

In the county court the proper officer will list the matter before the judge or district judge.[3]

Where 'family proceedings' are already pending, an application for an order under Part IV may be made on Form FL401 in those proceedings (i.e. the application could be made at the next date of hearing unless the court or justices' clerk as applicable considers that an earlier hearing would prevent delay or would otherwise be more convenient).[4]

---

[2] An intriguing situation arises whereby, if parties apply at the same time under both section 8 Children Act 1989 and Part IV Family Law Act 1996, then vis-à-vis section 8 the parties must *not* file statements with the application, but with regard to the Part IV application the applicant, in most cases, will have to file such a statement. This conflict — to which practitioners should be alert — is in practice remedied by the court giving specific directions relating to the filing of statements and affidavits.

[3] The various forms referred to in this section (and elsewhere in the chapter) are set out in an appendix to the relevant court rules. It is not possible to reproduce them all in this work.

[4] For the definition of family proceedings see s.8(3) and (4) Children Act 1989.

Ex parte applications: a note

An application on Form FL401 (above) may be made *ex parte*. In the family proceedings court the leave of the justices' clerk has to be obtained. There is no requirement for leave in the county court.

The applicant must file the application form with the justices' clerk or court at the time when the application is made (or at such time as directed) and the evidence in support of the application—and the applicant must state the reasons why the application is being made *ex parte* (rule 3A(4) FPC rules; rule 3.8(5) FPR rules) (and see section 45 Family Law Act 1996 below which sets out the circumstances to which the court is to have regard in deciding whether or not to exercise its powers on an *ex parte* application).

Although there is no requirement for an oral or written statement or affidavit showing *imminent danger* to be provided to justify an *ex parte* application it would appear from the wording of section 45 FLA 1996 that these should be the only circumstances in which an *ex parte* application ought to be made or granted unless it is either not reasonable and practicable to give notice or giving notice would give the respondent time to defeat the purpose of the application and it is likely that he or she would do so. Note that in the county court an affidavit is required whereas in the family proceedings court the evidence can be written or oral.

In accordance with former practice, *ex parte* applications and orders continue to be the exception. Section 45 represents the enactment of a line of cases which includes *Loseby v Newman* (1995) 2 FLR 754, *G v G (Ouster: Ex parte Application)* (1990) 1 FLR 395 and *Wookey v Wookey: Re S (A Minor)* (1991) 2 FLR 319:

(1) The court may, in any case where it considers that it is just and convenient to do so, make an occupation order or a non molestation order even though the respondent has not been given such notice of the proceedings as would otherwise be required by rules of court.

(2) In determining whether to exercise its powers under subsection (1), the court shall have regard to all the circumstances including -

(a) any risk of significant harm to the applicant or relevant child, attributable to conduct of the respondent, if the order was not made immediately;

(b) whether it is likely that the applivcant will be deterred or prevented from pursuine the application if the order is not made immediately;

(c) whether there is reson to believe that the responent is aware of the proceedings but is deliberately evading service and that the applicant or relevant child will be sriously prejudiced by the delay involved

(i) where the court is a magistrtes' court in effecting service of proceedings; or

(ii) in any other court, in effecting substituted service.

(3) if the court makes an order by virtue of subsection (1) it must afford the respondent an opportunity to make represntations relating to the order as soon as just and convenient at a full hearing.

Service of documents

Where the application is made on notice[5] the applicant is required to serve a copy on the respondent personally together with any written statement or affidavit supporting it, and of form FL402, at least two working days before the hearing (rule 3A(5) FPC rules; rule 3.8(6) FPR rules). Additionally, he or she must serve a copy of any application for an occupation order (where made under sections 33, 35 or 36 of the Family Law Act 1996: see *Chapter 3)* by first class post on the mortgagee or landlord of a dwelling house with a notice in Form FL416 informing him or her of his or her right to make representations in writing or at any hearing (rule 3A(10) FPC rules; rule 3.8(11) FPR rules). These relate to situations where the respondent has a legal right of occupation and the order could adversely affect the mortgagee/landlord.

The minimum two days for service may be reduced by the court or the justices' clerk (rule 3A(6) FPC rules; rule 3.8(7) FPR rules). There is no guidance in the 1996 Act or the rules as to when this discretion ought to be exercised. Case law suggests that upon an *ex parte* application the court should consider whether it would be more appropriate to require very short service rather than to proceed *ex parte* (*Wookey v Wookey*, above). In general, judges tend to regard it as preferable to adopt such a course as an alternative to proceeding straightaway 'in absence' because an expedited hearing on notice may lead to a reduction in the domestic tensions via an opportunity to explore the suitability of undertakings and underline the importance of compliance with any undertaking accepted or order granted (see also *G v G (Ouster: Ex Parte Application)* (1990)) above where it was said that *any* notice is better than non at all).

When an applicant is not legally represented in the family proceedings court, personal service may, with the leave of the justices' clerk, be dispensed with and instead service may be effected in accordance with rule 4 FPC rules (not reproduced in this work), i.e. by delivering the documents at or sending them by first class post to the respondent's residence or last known address; or where the respondent *is* legally represented, by delivering the documents at or sending them by first class post to his or her solicitor's address; or by sending them through a document exchange or by fax to that firm's address (rule 3A(7) FPC rules). Where the applicant is acting in person in the county court the service must be effected by the court on request (the county court can also order substituted service): rule 3.8(8) FPR rules.

---

[5] i.e. other than *ex parte*

In normal circumstances, following service of a copy of the application, the applicant must file a statement of service in Form FL 415.

Non-disclosure of addresses

An important power is contained in rule 33A Family Proceedings Courts (Children Act 1989) Rules 1991—which also applies to applications made on Form FL401—to prevent the disclosure of an address. If a party does wish to prevent his or her address being revealed, notice may be given to the court in writing and the address may not then be revealed except by order of the court. We emphasised the need for sensitivity to this aspect of domestic violence cases and the fact that it is a matter of general concern in earlier chapters. Court officials and practitioners need to take great care to ensure that this rule, when it applies, is not broken in error. Many courts use blue forms on the front of the case file to make it clear that non-disclosure applies to the case. See also *Confidentiality of documents*, below.

Answer/acknowledgement of service

Unlike certain applications under the Children Act 1989 (e.g. an application under s.8 of that Act for a private law order in respect of a child) there is *no* requirement under Part IV FLA 1996 for the respondent to serve an acknowledgement of service in the absence of a specific direction by the court for him or her to do so.

Directions

The power to give directions concerning cases under Part IV is very similar to that which exists under the Children Act 1989. Directions amount to instructions given by the court to the applicant and in due course to the other parties to the case. The main purpose is to give the court power to manage the case in an efficient, yet fair manner.

The rules give power to the justices' clerk or in the county court the district judge to give, vary or revoke directions for the conduct of proceedings including matters such as setting a time table, varying time periods, service of documents and the submission of evidence. However, unlike Children Act proceedings, in many simple non-molestation order cases the practice has developed since the FLA 1996 for courts to dispense with an initial formal directions hearing. However, if directions are given, Form FL404 should be used to notify the parties. Where the application does not seek to prevent actual physical or psychological violence by the respondent it may nonetheless be appropriate to list the matter for directions as soon as possible (subject to compliance with relevant notice periods) as the parties will be required to file statements in advance of any hearing (below) and attendance at a directions appointment always allows for the possibility or suitability of undertakings to be explored.

Documentary evidence

As already indicated above the parties are required to file and serve written statements (family proceedings court) or affidavits (county court) setting out the substance of the evidence upon which they intend to rely at the hearing. Such documents must be signed and dated, and contain an appropriate declaration as to the making of the statement or affidavit. Copies of any other documents upon which a party seeks to rely must also be filed and served. Failure to do this will lead to a party having to seek the leave of the justices' clerk or district judge in the case of a directions appointment, or the court in the case of a hearing, before he or she may give oral evidence or seek to rely on the document.

Oral evidence

The justices' clerk or the court as appropriate is obliged to keep a note of the substance of all oral evidence given at a hearing or directions appointment. There is a further requirement that records of hearings be made on form FL405 (rule 12A(1) FPC rules; rule 3.9(6) FPR rules).

The hearing and court orders

Before the hearing begins the magistrates must read any documents which have been filed (rule 12(1) FPC rules). In the county court the same requirement applies to the judge or district judge. Hearings in the county court will be 'in chambers' unless the court directs otherwise (rule 3.9(1) FPR rules). Directions may be given as to the order of speeches and evidence. In the absence of such directions the usual order is that the applicant goes first followed by the respondent and finally the child if he or she is also a respondent.

The court may direct that a further hearing be held to consider any representations made by a mortgagee or landlord (rule 12A(7) FPC rules; rule 3.9(7) FPR rules).

Justices' reasons and findings of fact must be recorded in writing and be stated by the court or by one of the justices before the court makes any order or refuses any application under the Act (rule 12(5) FPC rules). A justices' clerk is required to supply a copy of the reasons upon request to any person where he or she is satisfied that this is required in connection with an appeal or possible appeal (rule 12(8) FPC rules).[6]

The record of the hearing must be made on form FL405 Many courts place a 'seal' on such orders to minimise the risk of fraud or similar abuse. As already indicated above any order made on such application

---

[6] There is no equivalent statutory duty to give reasons in the county court.

must be made in form FL404. That form incorporates separate menus of possible orders (both non-molestation orders and occupation orders) and these menus operate as useful checklists for courts to see what can be ordered in each particular case.

Service of orders

The applicant is responsible for service of any order made on application on notice, i.e. *inter partes*, and the respondent must be served personally with any such order (rule 12A(5) FPC rules; rule 3.9(4) FPR rules).

Where the applicant is acting in person, he or she may, with leave of the justices' clerk, effect service in accordance with rule 4 FPC rules by:

- delivering the documents at or sending them by first class post to the respondent's residence or last known address; or
- where the respondent is represented, by delivering the documents at or sending them by first class post to his or her solicitor's address; or
- sending them through a document exchange or by fax to that firm's address.

In the county court, rule 3.9(5) FPR Rules allows an unrepresented applicant to ask the court to effect service of the order, when the court must then do so.

Additionally where the application is for an occupation order under s.33, 35 or 36 of the Family Law Act 1996 (all cases where the respondent has a legal right to occupy the house) a copy of any order made on that application must be served by the applicant by first class post on the mortgagee or (where relevant) the landlord (rule 12A(4) FPC rules; rule 3.9(3) FPR rules). It is unclear what is to happen if the applicant does not have details of the landlord or mortgagee (whichever is appropriate) but as service of the notice is a mandatory requirement the applicant should presumably use his or her best endeavours to obtain details and provide a full account of the steps taken. There would then appear to be no reason why directions could not be made regarding the service of this notice in the circumstances.

An order made on an *ex parte* application must be served by the applicant together with a copy of the application and, as the case may be, the statement or affidavit supporting it on the respondent personally (rule 12A(2) FPC rules; rule 3.9(2) FPR rules). However, if the applicant is acting in person a copy of such an order made on an *ex parte* application must, in the family proceedings court, be served by the justices' clerk or county court a applicable if the applicant requests this (rule 12A(3) FPC rules; rule 3.9(5) FPR rules). Indeed it may be appropriate for the justices' clerk or court to suggest that he, she or the court take responsibility for service in such circumstances (especially, e.g. when an *ex parte* order has been made on account of the respondent's violence)—as such action may in itself reduce the danger of any repetition.

Applicatons to vary, etc. orders made under Part IV FLA 1996

Any application to vary, extend or discharge an order made under Part IV of the 1996 Act must be made in form FL403 and to the court which made the order.

Costs

The court may order one party to the proceedings under the Family Law Act 1996 to pay the costs of the other, but the party against whom the court is considering making the order must be given the opportunity to make representations.

Confidentiality of documents

Leave of the justices' clerk or the court is required before documents (other than a record of an order) relating to proceedings may be disclosed to anyone other than a party, that party's legal representative or the Legal Aid Board. The same comments apply here as we have made in relation to confidentiality generally: courts should be meticulous in this regard.

Legal aid considerations

Changes to the legal aid position regarding applications under Part IV have reduced any financial incentive for solicitors to have cases under Part IV dealt with in the county court as there is now a system of fixed fees in the county court and the family proceedings court. At the same time, however, the Legal Aid Board now no longer limits legal aid certificates in simple cases to the family proceedings court.

Fees

No fee is payable for an application in the family proceedings court. A fee of £40 (July 1999) is payable in respect of applications in the county court.

Materials: Chapter 5

ALLOCATION OF CASES

The Family Law Act 1996 (Part IV) (Allocation of Proceedings Order) 1997[7]: Key Extracts

This Order provides for the allocation of proceedings under Part IV of the Family Law Act 1996 (Family Homes and Domestic Violence) between the High Court, the county courts and the magistrates' courts. Article 4(2) prescribes those proceedings which must be commenced in the High Court and article 5 the courts in which are to be brought applications to vary, extend or discharge orders. Articles 6 to 15 regulate transfer between different courts and categories of courts. Article 16 provides for the Principal Registry of the Family Division to be treated as a county court and article 17 provides for proceedings to be taken in Lambeth, Shoreditch and Woolwich county courts. Article 18 makes provision in relation to proceedings which are commenced or transferred in contravention of the Order.

. . . .

COMMENCEMENT OF PROCEEDINGS

Commencement of proceedings

4. — (1) Subject to section 59, paragraph 1 of Schedule 7 and the provisions of this article, proceedings under Part IV may be commenced in a county court or in a family proceedings court.

    (2) An application

    (a) under Part IV brought by an applicant who is under the age of eighteen; and

    (b) for the grant of leave under section 43 (Leave of court required for applications by children under sixteen), shall be commenced in the High Court.

    (3) Where family proceedings are pending in a county court or a family proceedings court, an application under Part IV may be made in those proceedings.

Application to extend, vary or discharge order

5. — (1) Proceedings under Part IV

    (a) to extend, vary or discharge an order, or

    (b) the determination of which may have the effect of varying or discharging an order, shall be made to the court which made the order.

---

[7] SI 1891/1997

(2) A court may transfer proceedings made in accordance with paragraph (1) to any other court in accordance with the provisions of articles 6 to 14.

TRANSFER OF PROCEEDINGS

Disapplication of enactments about transfer
6. Sections 38 and 39 of the Matrimonial and Family Proceedings Act 1984 shall not apply to proceedings under Part IV.

Transfer from one family proceedings court to another
7. A family proceedings court ('the transferring court') shall (on application or of its own motion) transfer proceedings under Part IV to another family proceedings court ('the receiving court') where it considers that -
- (a) the transferring court considers that it would be appropriate for those proceedings to be heard together with other family proceedings which are pending in the receiving court; and
- (b) the receiving court, by its justices' clerk (as defined by rule 1(2) of the Family Proceedings Courts (Children Act 1989) Rules 1991), consents to the transfer.

Transfer from family proceedings court to county court
8. — (1) A family proceedings court may, on application or of its own motion, transfer proceedings under Part IV to a county court where it considers that -
- (a) it would be appropriate for those proceedings to be heard together with other family proceedings which are pending in that court; or
- (b) the proceedings involve
  - (i) a conflict with the law of another jurisdiction;
  - (ii) some novel and difficult point of law;
  - (iii) some question of general public interest; or
  - (vi) the proceedings are exceptionally complex.

(2) A family proceedings court must transfer proceedings under Part IV to a county court where -
- (a) a child under the age of eighteen is the respondent to the application or wishes to become a party to the proceedings; or
- (b) a party to the proceedings is a person who, by reason of mental disorder within the meaning of the Mental Health Act 1983, is incapable of managing and administering his property and affairs.

(3) Except where transfer is ordered under paragraph (1)(a), the proceedings shall be transferred to the nearest county court.

Transfer from family proceedings court to High Court
9. A family proceedings court may, on application or of its own motion, transfer proceedings under Part IV to the High Court where it considers that it would be appropriate for those proceedings to be heard together with other family proceedings which are pending in that Court.

Transfer from one county court to another

10. A county court may, on application or of its own motion, transfer proceedings under Part IV to another county court where

- (a) it considers that it would be appropriate for those proceedings to be heard together with other family proceedings which are pending in that court;
- (b) the proceedings involve the determination of a question of a kind mentioned in section 59(1) and the property in question is situated in the district of another county court; or
- (c) it seems necessary or expedient so to do.

Transfer from county court to family proceedings court

11. A county court may, on application or of its own motion, transfer proceedings under Part IV to family proceedings court where

- (a) it considers that it would be appropriate for those proceedings to be heard together with other family proceedings which are pending in that court; or
- (b) it considers that the criterion
  (i) in article 8(1)(a) no longer applies because the proceedings with which the transferred proceedings were to be heard have been determined;
  (ii) in article 8(1)(b) or (c) does not apply.

Transfer from county court to High Court

12. A county court may, on application or of its own motion, transfer proceedings under Part IV to the High Court where it considers that the proceedings are appropriate for determination in the High Court.

Transfer from High Court to family proceedings court

13. The High Court may, on application or of its own motion, transfer proceedings under Part IV to a family proceedings court where it considers that it would be appropriate for those proceedings to be heard together with other family proceedings which are pending in that court.

Transfer from High Court to county court

14. The High Court may, on application or of its own motion, transfer proceedings under Part IV to a county court where it considers that -

- (a) it would be appropriate for those proceedings to be heard together with other family proceedings which are pending in that court;
- (b) the proceedings are appropriate for determination in a county court; or
- (c) it is appropriate for an application made by a child under the age of eighteen to be heard in a county court

Disposal following arrest

15. Where a person is brought before -

- (a) a relevant judicial authority in accordance with section 47(7)(a), or
- (b) a court by virtue of a warrant issued under section 47(9),

and the matter is not disposed of forthwith, the matter may be transferred to be disposed of by the relevant judicial authority or court which issued the warrant or, as the case may be, which attached the power of arrest under section 47(2) or (3) if different.

MISCELLANEOUS

Principal Registry of the Family Division
16. — (1) The principal registry of the Family Division of the High Court shall be treated, for the purposes of this Order, as if it were a divorce county court, a family hearing centre and a care centre.

(2) Without prejudice to article 10, the principal registry may transfer an order made in proceedings which are pending in the principal registry to the High Court for enforcement.

Lambeth, Shoreditch and Woolwich County Courts
17. Proceedings under Part IV may be commenced in, transferred to and tried in Lambeth, Shoreditch and Woolwich County Court.

Contravention of provisions of this Order
18. Where proceedings are commenced or transferred in contravention of a provision of this Order, the contravention shall not have the effect of making the proceedings invalid.

APPLICATION FORM

FORM FL401

Application for:	**To be completed by the court**
— a non-molestation order	Date issued
— an occupation order	

(Family Law Act Part IV)   Case number EG/1000/99/0

The court   Roddenbury Family Proceedings Court

Please read the accompanying notes as you complete this form

1 About you (the applicant)
State your title (Mr, Mrs etc.), full name,address, telephone number and date of birth (if under 18):

Mrs. Maggie Straight, 1 Courthouse Road, Roddenbury

State your solicitor's name, address, reference, telephone, FAX and DX numbers:

```
Smith and Co, Market Square,
Roddenbury    D.o.b. 8.8.64
```

2 About the respondent

State the respondent's name, address and date of birth (if known):

```
Sly Pendry, Crown Court Avenue,
London    D.o.b. 6.1.62
```

3 The Order(s) for which you are applying

This application is for:

☐ a non-molestation order

☐ an occupation order

☐ Tick this box if you wish the court to hear your application without notice being given to the respondent. The reasons relied on for an application being heard without notice must be stated in the statement in support.

4 Your relationship to the respondent (the person to be served with this application)

Your relationship to the respondent is:
Please tick only one of the following

1 ☐ Married
2 ☐ Were married
3 ☐ Cohabiting
4 ☐ Were cohabiting

5 ☐ Both of you live or have lived in the same household

6 ☐ Relative
   State how related:

7 ☐ Agreed to marry.
   Give the date the agreement was made.
   If the agreement has ended, state when.

8 ☐ Both of you are parents of or have parental responsibility for a child

9 ☐ One of you is a parent of a child and the other has parental responsibility for that child

10☐ One of you is the natural parent or grandparent of a child adopted or freed for adoption, and the other is:
      (i) the adoptive parent
or (ii) a person who has applied for an adoption order for the child
or (iii) a person with whom the child has been placed for adoption
or (iv) the child who has been adopted or freed for adoption.
State whether (i), (ii), (iii) or (iv):

11 ☐ Both of you are parties to the same family proceedings (see also Section 11 below).

5 Application for a non-molestation order

If you wish to apply for a non-molestation order, state briefly in this section the order you want.

Give full details in support of your application in your supporting evidence

An order that the respondent be forbidden from molesting, from harassing, pestering or assaulting the applicant.

Power of arrest.

6 Application for an occupation order

If you do not wish to apply for an occupation order please go to section 9 of this form.

(A) State the address of the dwelling house to which your application relates:

1 Courthouse Road, Roddenbury

(B) State whether it is occupied by you or
the respondent now or in the past, or
whether it was intended to be occupied
by you or the respondent:

Occupied by self and respondent since Nov 1998.

(C) State whether you are entitled to occupy
the dwelling-house: □ Yes   □ No

If yes, explain why: Tenancy in my sole name

(D) State whether the respondent is entitled
to occupy the dwelling-house:
□ Yes   □ No

If yes, explain why: See above

**On the basis of your answer to (C) and
(D) above, tick one of the boxes 1 to 5
below to show the category into which
you fit**

1 □ a spouse who has matrimonial home
rights in the dwelling-house, or a person
who is entitled to occupy it by virtue of
a beneficial estate or interest or contract
or by virtue of any enactment giving
him or her the right to remain in
occupation. **There is no dispute
about occupation.**

If you tick box 1, state whether there is a
dispute or pending proceedings
between you and the respondent about
your right to occupy the dwelling-
house.

2 □ a former spouse with no existing right
to occupy, where the respondent spouse
is entitled.

3 □ a cohabitant or former cohabitant with
no existing right to occupy, where the
respondent cohabitant or former
cohabitant is so entitled.

4 ☐ a spouse or former spouse who is not entitled to occupy, where the respondent spouse or former spouse is also not entitled.

5 ☐ a cohabitant or former cohabitant who is not entitled to occupy, where the respondent cohabitant or former cohabitant is also not entitled.

Matrimonial Home Rights

If you do have matrimonial home rights please:
State whether the title to the land is registered or unregistered (if known):

If registered, state the Land Registry title number (if known):

If you wish to apply for an occupation order, state briefly here the order you want. Give full details in support of your application in your supporting evidence.

7 Application for additional order(s) about the dwelling house

If you want to apply for any of the orders listed in the notes to this section, state what order you would like the court to make:

8 Mortgage and rent

Is the dwelling house subject to a mortgage?

☐ Yes ☐ No

If yes, please provide the name and address of the mortgagee:

Is the dwelling house rented?

☐ Yes ☐ No

If yes, please provide the name and address of the landlord:

9 At the court

Will you need an interpreter at court?

☐ Yes   ☐ No
If 'Yes', specify the language:

If you need an interpreter because you do not speak English, you are responsible for providing your own.

If you need an interpreter or other facilities because of a disability, please contact the court to ask what help is available.

10 Other information

State the name and date of birth of any child living with or staying with, or likely to live with or stay with, you or the respondent:
State the name of any other person living in the same household as you and the respondent, and say why they live there:

11 Other Proceedings and Orders

If there are any other current family proceedings or orders in force involving you and the respondent, state the type of proceedings or orders, the court and the case number. This includes any application for an occupation order or non-molestation order against you by the respondent.

This application is to be served upon the respondent

Signed   Date

Application for a Non-molestation Order or Occupation Order

Notes for Guidance

Section 1

If you do not wish your address to be made known to the respondent leave the space on the form blank and complete Confidential Address Form C8. The court can give you this form.

If you are under 18 someone over 18 must help you make this application. That person, who might be one of your parents, is called a 'next friend'.

If you are under 16 you need permission to make this application. You must apply to the High Court for permission, using this form. If the High Court gives you permission to make this application, it will then either hear the application itself or transfer it to a county court.

Section 3

An urgent order made by the court before notice of the application is served on the respondent is called an ex-parte order. In deciding whether to make an ex-parte order the court will consider all the circumstances of the case including:

- *any risk of significant harm to the applicant or a relevant child, attributable to conduct of the respondent, if the order is not made immediately*
- *whether it is likely that the applicant will be deterred or prevented from pursuing the application if an order is not made immediately*
- *whether there is reason to believe that the respondent is aware of the proceedings but is deliberately evading service and that the applicant or a relevant child will be seriously prejudiced by the delay involved*

If the court makes an ex-parte order, it must give the respondent an opportunity to make representations about the order as soon as just and convenient at a full hearing.

'Harm' in relation to a person who has reached the age of 18 means ill-treatment or the impairment of health, and in relation to a child means ill-treatment or the impairment of health and development.

'Ill-treatment' includes forms of ill-treatment which are not physical and, in relation to a child, includes sexual abuse. The court will require evidence of any harm which you allege in support of your application. This evidence should be included in the statement accompanying this application.

Section 4

For you to be able to apply for an order you must be related to the respondent in one of the ways listed in this section of the form. If you are not related in one of these ways you should seek legal advice.

Cohabitants *are a man and a woman who although not married to each other are living or have lived together as husband and wife. People who have cohabited but have then married will not fall within this category, but will fall within the category of married people.*

Those who live or have lived in the same household *do not include people who share the same household because one of them is the other's employee, tenant, lodger or boarder.*

You will only be able to apply as a relative of the respondent if you are:
(A) the father, mother, step-father, step-mother, son, daughter, step-son, step-daughter, grandmother, grandfather, grandson or granddaughter of the respondent or of the respondent's spouse or former spouse.
(B) the brother, sister, uncle, aunt, niece or nephew (whether of the full blood or of the half blood or by marriage) of the respondent or of the respondent's spouse or former spouse.

This includes, in relation to a person who is living or has lived with another person as husband and wife, any person who would fall within (A) or (B) if the parties were married to each other (for example your cohabitee's father or brother).

Agreements to marry: You will fall within this category only if you make this application within three years of the termination of the agreement. The court will require the following evidence of the agreement:

> evidence in writing
> **or** the gift of an engagement ring in contemplation of marriage
> **or** evidence that a ceremony has been entered into in the presence of
>> one or more other persons assembled for the purpose of witnessing it.

Parents and parental responsibility: You will fall within this category if

> both you and the respondent are either the parents of a child or have parental responsibility for that child
> **or** if one of you is the parent and the other has parental responsibility.

Under the Children Act 1989, parental responsibility is held automatically by a child's mother, and by the child's father if he and the mother were married to each other at the time of the child's birth or have married subsequently. Where this is not the case, parental responsibility can be acquired by the father in accordance with the provisions of the Children Act 1989.

Section 5

A non-molestation order can forbid the respondent to molest you or a relevant child. Molestation can include, for example, violence, threats, pestering and other forms of harassment. The court can forbid particular acts of the respondent, molestation in general, or both.

Section 6

If you wish to apply for an occupation order but you are uncertain about your answer to any of the questions in this part of the application form, you should seek legal advice.

(A) A dwelling-house includes any building or part of a building which is occupied as a dwelling; any caravan, houseboat or structure which is occupied as a dwelling; and any yard, garden, garage or outhouse belonging to it and occupied with it.

(C) & (D) *The following questions give examples to help you to decide if you or the respondent, or both of you, are entitled to occupy the dwelling-house:*

(a) Are you the sole legal owner of the dwelling-house?
(b) Are you and the respondent joint legal owners of the dwelling house?
(c) Is the respondent the sole legal owner of the dwelling-house?
(d) Do you rent the dwelling-house as sole tenant?
(e) Do you and the respondent rent the dwelling-house as joint tenants?
(f) Does the respondent rent the dwelling house as sole tenant?

If you answer
- **Yes** to (a), (b), (d) or (e) you are likely to be entitled to occupy the dwelling-house

- **Yes** to (c) or (f) you may not be entitled (unless, for example, you are a spouse and have matrimonial home rights - see the notes under 'Matrimonial Home Rights' below)

- **Yes** to (b), (c), (e), or (f) the respondent is likely to be entitled to occupy the dwelling-house

- **Yes** to (a) or (d) the respondent may not be entitled (unless for example, he is a spouse and has matrimonial home rights).

Box 1 For example, if you are sole owner, joint owner, or if you rent the property. If you are not a spouse, former spouse, cohabitant or former cohabitant of the respondent, you will only be able to apply for an occupation order if you fall within this category.

If you answer **Yes** to this question, it will not be possible for a magistrates' court to deal with the application, unless the court decides that it is unnecessary for it to decide this question in order to deal with the application or make an order. If the court decides that it cannot deal with the application it will transfer the application to a county court.

Box 2 For example if the respondent was married to you and is sole owner or rents the property.

Box 3 *For example if the respondent is or was cohabiting with you and is sole owner or rents the property.*

Matrimonial Home Rights

Where one spouse is entitled to occupy the dwelling-house by virtue of a beneficial estate or interest or contract or by virtue of any enactment giving him or her the right to remain in occupation, and the other spouse is not so entitled, the spouse who is not entitled has matrimonial home rights. These are a right, if the spouse is in occupation, not to be evicted or excluded from the dwelling house except with the leave of the court and, if the spouse is not in occupation, the right with the leave of the court to enter into and occupy the dwelling-house.

Matrimonial home rights do not exist if the dwelling-house has never been, and was never intended to be, the matrimonial home of the two spouses. If the marriage has come to an end, matrimonial home rights will also have ceased, unless a court order has been made during the marriage for the rights to continue after the end of the marriage.

Occupation Orders *The possible orders are:*

If you have ticked box 1 above, an order under section 33 of the Act may:

- *enforce the applicant's entitlement to remain in occupation as against the respondent*
- *require the respondent to permit the applicant to enter and remain in the dwelling-house or part of it*
- *regulate the occupation of the dwelling-house by either or both parties*
- *if the respondent is also entitled to occupy, the order may prohibit, suspend or restrict the exercise by him, of that right*
- *restrict or terminate any matrimonial home rights of the respondent*
- *require the respondent to leave the dwelling-house or part of it*
- *exclude the respondent from a defined area around the dwelling-house*
- *declare that the applicant is entitled to occupy the dwelling-house or has matrimonial home rights in it*
- *provide that matrimonial home rights of the applicant are not brought to an*

end by the death of the other spouse or termination of the marriage.

If you have ticked box 2 or box 3 above, on order under section 35 or 36 of the Act may:

- *give the applicant the right not to be evicted or excluded from the dwelling-house or any part of it by the respondent for a specified period*
- *prohibit the respondent from evicting or excluding the applicant during that period*
- *give the applicant the right to enter and occupy the dwelling-house for a specified period*
- *require the respondent to permit the exercise of that right*
- *regulate the occupation of the dwelling-house by either or both of the parties*
- *prohibit, suspend or restrict the exercise by the respondent of his right to occupy*
- *require the respondent to leave the dwelling-house or part of it*
- *exclude the respondent from a defined area around the dwelling house.*

If you have ticked box 4 or box 5 above, an order under section 37 or 38 of the Act may:

- *require the respondent to permit the applicant to enter and remain in the dwelling-house or part of it*
- *regulate the occupation of the dwelling-house by either or both of the parties*
- *require the respondent to leave the dwelling-house or part of it*
- *exclude the respondent from a defined area around the dwelling-house.*

You should provide any evidence which you have on the following matters in your evidence in support of this application. If necessary, further statements may be submitted after the application has been issued

If you have ticked box 1, 4 or 5 above, the court will need any available evidence of the following:

- *the housing needs and resources of you, the respondent and any relevant child*
- *the financial resources of you and the respondent*

- the likely effect of any order or of any decision not to make an order on the health, safety and well-being of you, the respondent and any relevant child
- the conduct of you and the respondent in relation to each other and otherwise.

If you have ticked box 2 above, the court will need any available evidence of:

- the housing needs and resources of you the respondent and relevant child
- the financial resources of you and the respondent
- the likely effect of any order or of any decision not to make an order on the health, safety and well-being of you, the respondent and any relevant child
- the conduct of you and the respondent in relation to each other and otherwise
- the length of time that has elapsed since you and the respondent ceased to live together
- the length of time that has elapsed since the marriage was dissolved or annulled
- the existence of any pending proceedings between you and the respondent:
  under section 23A of the Matrimonial Causes Act 1973 (property adjustment orders in connection with divorce proceedings etc.
  or under Schedule 1 para 1(2)(d) or (e) of the Children Act 1989 (orders for financial relief against parents)
  or relating to the legal or beneficial ownership of the dwelling-house.

If you have ticked box 3 above, the court will need any available evidence of:

- the housing needs and resources of you, the respondent and any relevant child
- the financial resources of you and the respondent
- the likely effect of any order, or of any decision not to make an order, on the health, safety and well-being of you, the respondent and any relevant child
- the conduct of you and the respondent in relation to each other and otherwise
- the nature of you and the respondent's relationship

- the length of time which you have lived together as husband and wife
- whether you and the respondent have had any children or have both had parental responsibility for any children
- the length of time which has elapsed since you and the respondent ceased to live together
- the existence of any pending proceedings between you and the respondent under Schedule 1 para 1(2)(d) or (e) of the Children Act 1989 or relating to the legal or beneficial ownership of the dwelling-house.

Section 7

Under section 40 of the Act the court may make the following additional orders when making an occupation order:

- impose on either party obligations as to the repair and maintenance of the dwelling-house
- impose on either party obligations as to the payment of rent, mortgage or other outgoings affecting it
- order a party occupying the dwelling-house to make periodical payments to the other party in respect of the accommodation, if the other party would (but for the order) be entitled to occupy it
- grant either party possession or use of furniture or other contents
- order either party to take reasonable care of any furniture or other contents
- order either party to take reasonable steps to keep the dwelling-house and any furniture or other contents secure.

Section 8

If the dwelling-house is rented or subject to a mortgage the landlord or mortgagee must be served with notice of the proceedings in Form FL416. He or she will then be able to make representations to the court regarding the rent or mortgage.

Section 10

A person living in the same household may, for example, be a member of the family or a tenant or employee of you or the respondent.

RULES OF PROCEDURE: KEY EXTRACTS

Magistrates' Courts
The Family Proceedings Courts (Matrimonial Proceedings etc.) Rules 1991[7]

Applications under Part IV of the Family Law Act 1996

3(A) – (1) An application for an occupation order or a non-molestation order under Part IV of the Family Law Act 1996 (Family Homes and Domestic Violence) shall be made in Form FL401.

(2) An application for an occupation order or a non-molestation order which is made in other proceedings which are pending shall be made in Form FL401.

(3) An application in Form FL401 shall be supported -

(a) by a statement which is signed and is declared to be true; or

(b) with the leave of the court, by oral evidence.

(4) An application in Form FL401 may, with the leave of the justices' clerk or of the court, be made ex parte, in which case

(a) the applicant shall file with the justices' clerk or the court the application at the time when the application is made or as directed by the justices' clerk; and

(b) the evidence in support of the application shall state the reasons why the application is made ex parte.

(5) An application made on notice (together with any statement supporting it and a notice in Form FL402) shall be served by the applicant on the respondent personally not less than two days prior to the date on which the application will be heard.

(6) The court or the justices' clerk may abridge the period specified in paragraph (5).

(7) Where the applicant is acting in person, service of the application may, with the leave of the justices' clerk, be effected in accordance with rule 4.

(8) Where an application for an occupation order or a non-molestation order is pending the court shall consider (on the application of either party or of its own motion) whether to exercise its powers to transfer the hearing of that application to another court and the justices' clerk or the court shall make an order for transfer in Form FL417 if it seems necessary or expedient to do so.

(9) Where an order for transfer is made, the justices clerk shall send a copy of the order -

(a) to the parties, and

(b) to the family proceedings court or to the county court to which the proceedings are to be transferred.

(10) A copy of an application for an occupation order under section 33, 35 or 36 of the Family Law Act 1996 shall be served by the applicant by first-class post

---

[7] SI 1991/1991 as amended – including by the Family Proceedings Courts (Matrimonial Proceedings etc.) (Amendment) Rules 1997: effective 1 October 1997

on the mortgagee or, as the case may be, the landlord of the dwelling-house in question, with a notice in Form FLA416 informing him of his right to make representations in writing or at any hearing.

(11) The applicant shall file a statement in Form FL415 after he has served the application.

(12) Rule 33A of the Family Proceedings Courts (Children Act 1989) Rules 1991 (disclosure of addresses) shall apply for the purpose of preventing the disclosure of addresses where an application is made in Form FL401 as it applies for that purpose in proceedings under the Children Act 1989

. . . . .

Hearing of applications under Part IV of the Family Law Act 1996

12A. – (1) This rule applies to the hearing of applications under Part IV of the Family Law Act 1996 and the following forms shall be used in connection with such hearings:

(a) a record of the hearing shall be made on Form FL405, and

(b) any order made on the hearing shall be issued in Form FL404.

(2) Where an order is made on an application made ex parte, a copy of the order together with a copy of the application and of any statement supporting it shall be served by the applicant on the respondent personally.

(3) Where the applicant is acting in person, service of a copy of an order made on an application made ex parte shall be effected by the justices' clerk if the applicant so requests.

(4) Where the application is for an occupation order under section 33, 35 or 36 of the Family Law Act 1996, a copy of any order made on the application shall be served by the applicant by first class post on the mortgagee or, as the case may be, the landlord of the dwelling-house in question.

(5) A copy of an order made on an application heard inter partes shall be served by the applicant on the respondent personally.

(6) Where the applicant is acting in person, service of a copy of the order made on an application heard inter partes may, with the leave of the justices' clerk, be effected in accordance with rule 4.

(7) The court may direct that a further hearing be held in order to consider any representations made by a mortgagee or a landlord.

Applications to vary etc orders made under Part IV of the Family Law Act 1996

12B. An application to vary, extend or discharge an order made under Part IV of the Family Law Act 1996 shall be made in Form FL403 and rules 12 and 12A shall apply to the hearing of such an application.

. . . .

Setting aside on failure of service

24. Where an application has been sent to a respondent in accordance with rule 4(1) and, after an order has been made on the application, it appears to the court that the application did not come to the knowledge of the respondent in due

time, the court may of its own motion set aside the order and may give such directions as it thinks fit for the rehearing of the application.

. . . .

County Courts
Family Proceedings
Supreme Court of England and Wales

The Family Proceedings Rules 1991 [9]

Applications under Part IV of the Family Law Act 1996 (Family Homes and Domestic Violence)

3.8 — (1) An application for an occupation order or a non-molestation order under Part IV of the Family Law Act 1996 shall be made in Form FL401.

(2) An application for an occupation order or a non-molestation order made by a child under the age of sixteen shall be made in Form FL401 but shall be treated, in the first instance, as an application to the High Court for leave.

(3) An application for an occupation order or a non-molestation order which is made in other proceedings which are pending shall be made in Form FL401.

(4) An application in Form FL401 shall be supported by a statement which is signed by the applicant and is sworn to be true.

(5) Where an application is made without giving notice, the sworn statement shall state the reasons why notice was not given.

(6) An application made on notice (together with the sworn statement and a notice in Form FL402) shall be served by the applicant on the respondent personally not less than 2 days before the date on which the application will be heard.

(7) The court may abridge the period specified in paragraph (6).

(8) Where the applicant is acting in person, service of the application shall be effected by the court if the applicant so requests.

This does not affect the court's power to order substituted service.

(9) Where an application for an occupation order or a non-molestation order is pending, the court shall consider (on the application of either party or of its own motion) whether to exercise its powers to transfer the hearing of that application to another court and shall make an order for transfer in Form FL417 if it seems necessary or expedient to do so.

(10) Rule 9.2A shall not apply to an application for an occupation order or a non-molestation order under Part IV of the Family Law Act 1996.

(11) A copy of an application for an occupation order under section 33, 35 or 36 of the Family Law Act 1996 shall be served by the applicant by first-class post on the mortgagee or, as the case may be, the landlord of the dwelling-house in question, with a notice in Form FL416 informing him of his right to make representations in writing or at any hearing.

---

[9] Key amendments effected by the the Family Proceedings (Amendment No.3) Rules 1997 (SI 1893/1997)

(12) Where the application is for the transfer of a tenancy, notice of the application shall be served by the applicant on the other cohabitant or spouse and on the landlord (as those terms are defined by paragraph 1 of Schedule 7 to the Family Law Act 1996) and any person so served shall be entitled to be heard on the application.

(13) Rules 2.62(4) to (6) and 2.63 (investigation, requests for further information) shall apply, with the necessary modifications, to

(a) an application for an occupation order under section 33, 35 or 36 of the Family Law Act 1996, and

(b) an application for the transfer of a tenancy, as they apply to an application for ancillary relief.

(14) Rule 3.6(7) to (9) (Married Women's Property Act 1882) shall apply, with the necessary modifications, to an application for the transfer of a tenancy, as they apply to an application under rule 3.6.

(15) The applicant shall file a statement in Form FL415 after he has served the application.

Hearing of applications under Part IV of the Family Law Act 1996

3.9 — (1) An application for an occupation order or a non-molestation order under Part IV of the Family Law Act 1996 shall be dealt with in chambers unless the court otherwise directs.

(2) Where an order is made on an application made ex parte, a copy of the order together with a copy of the application and of the sworn statement in support shall be served by the applicant on the respondent personally.

(3) Where the application is for an occupation order under section 33, 35 or 36 of the Family Law Act 1996, a copy of any order made on the application shall be served by the applicant by first-class post on the mortgagee or, as the case may be, the landlord of the dwelling-house in question.

(4) A copy of an order made on an application heard inter partes shall be served by the applicant on the respondent personally.

(5) Where the applicant is acting in person, service of a copy of any order made on the hearing of the application shall be effected by the court if the applicant so requests.

(6) The following forms shall be used in connection with hearings of applications under Part IV of the Family Law Act 1996 -

(a) a record of the hearing shall be made on Form FL405, and

(b) any order made on the hearing shall be issued in Form FL404.

(7) The court may direct that a further hearing be held in order to consider any representations made by a mortgagee or a landlord.

(8) An application to vary, extend or discharge an order made under Part IV of the Family Law Act 1996 shall be made in Form FL403 and this rule shall apply to the hearing of such an application.

CHAPTER 6

Enforcement

Procedures for enforcing the remedies outlined in this book are either of a general nature or specific to the individual remedy. In some cases, they are, in effect, an integral part of a particular topic whereas in others they can be conveniently discussed separately. The position is as follows:

- criminal sanctions are of the variety applied to criminal matters in general with the single exception of the restraining order which is unique to harassment. Apart from the initial sentence, if, say, a fine, compensation order or condition of a probation order (say to take part in domestic violence sessions) needs to be enforced then this is done using standard enforcement procedures which it would be out of proportion to the main subject matter of this book to describe here. In the main and by one route or another an offender who does not comply with a criminal sentence is likely, ultimately, to risk imprisonment. For a summary see *The Sentence of the Court*, Watkins et al, Waterside Press, 1999. The special situation in relation to harassment is outlined in *Chapter 7*.

- similarly, proceedings under the ordinary civil jurisdiction of the county court and High Court are a matter of general import and the remedy is normally proceedings for contempt of court if, say, an injunction is not obeyed. Again, this may lead to imprisonment—but it should be noted that the standard of proof for breach of an injunction is 'beyond reasonable doubt'. A special situation arises under the Protection From Harassment Act 1997 which provides for civil sanctions under that Act to be enforced under the criminal law—but this is still not in force at the time of writing: see *Chapter 7*. Until then, harassment injunctions fall to be enforced by way of contempt. Contempt is sometimes used by judges to compel performance and to keep a matter under review by way of an adjournment or series of adjournments. Normally, if a civil matter falls to be enforced in the magistrates' court then, again, there are general provisions specific to that court (see later).

- special enforcement procedures apply to both non-molestation orders and occupation orders in High Court and the county court. For consistency, these are 'overlaid' on the standard magistrates' court civil enforcement powers. Enforcement under Part IV Family Law Act 1996 is outlined in this chapter.

ENFORCEMENT OF PART IV ORDERS

The rules relating to enforcement of non-molestation orders and occupation orders were designed to introduce a common approach to enforcement in all family courts. They are loosely based on the system operating in the county court prior to October 1997. There are a number of procedural safeguards to ensure that injustice is not done to the respondent. Despite this move towards consistency, the basic law governing enforcement of family proceedings court orders is still contained in section 63 Magistrates' Courts Act 1980 which provides for a maximum penalty in such courts of two months imprisonment (with the right to suspend this on such terms as the court thinks fit) or a fine of £50 per day of default up to a maximum of £5,000. Section 63 is set out later in the chapter. Note again that ordinary magistrates' courts can deal with enforcement matters unless these proceedings have been designated locally as family proceedings (p.87). Key questions where it is alleged an order has been breached are:

- how to get a respondent to court; and

- what powers exist when a breach or default is established to the satisfaction of the court.

The key procedures are contained in:

- the Family Proceedings Rules 1991 (as amended by the Family Proceedings (Amendment No. 3) Rules 1997) (described in this work as the 'FPR rules'); the County Court Rules (CCR); and the Rules of the Supreme Court (RSC)—all so far as the *county court* is concerned; and

- the Family Proceedings Courts (Matrimonial Proceedings etc.) Rules 1991 (as amended by the Family Procedings Court (Matrimonial Proceedings etc.) (Amendment) Rules 1997) in respect of the *family proceedings court* (the 'FPC rules').);

Key extracts from these rules are reproduced at the end of this chapter.

WHERE A POWER OF ARREST IS ATTACHED

As indicated in *Chapter 3*, section 47 Family Law Act 1996 makes it clear that a power of arrest should normally be attached to a non-molestation or occupation order when violence or threats of violence have been proved unless the court considers this unnecessary.

When such a power *is* attached to an order, the court—in addition to drafting an order using form FL404 (*Chapter 5*)—must insert those provisions of the order which are subject to the power of arrest in a separate form, FL406. Such provisions must be set out in individual clauses and must not refer to any behaviour which would not entitle a constable to arrest the respondent. County courts—in accordance with longstanding practice—generally only attach a power of arrest to non-molestation orders which forbid actual or threatened violence and not to orders covering general molestation or to orders which simply regulate the family home. This practice is now also being followed by most family proceedings courts. However there is no *statutory* restriction on the nature of the molestation order or occupation order to which a power of arrest may be attached.

Notification to the respondent and the police

Having drafted the orders, the two forms FL404 and FL406 must be delivered to the officer in charge of any police station covering the respondent's address or such other police station as the court has specified. Arrangements have been made in many areas of England and Wales between the courts and the police for certain 'divisional HQ' police stations to be specified for the purposes of the delivery of such forms.

The practice of the courts varies as to whether the court or the applicant takes responsibility for delivering these forms to the police station. Practitioners need to check out the local practice.

The police must also be served with a statement that a copy of the actual order in form FL404 has been served on the respondent or that he or she has been informed of the terms of the order. Again the rules are not clear on who will provide this statement, but in most cases it will be the applicant who in the majority of cases will be responsible for the service of the order on the respondent. In some cases, if the respondent appeared before the court, the court itself might provide a statement for the police that the respondent is actually aware of the provisions of the order.

Where an order to which a power of arrest has been attached is either varied or discharged, the rules (rule 20(2) FPC rules; rule 3.9A FPR rules) specify that it is the justices' clerk or the proper officer of the county court who must immediately inform the police station for the area in which the applicant resides, whether that is the police station originally provided with a copy of the power of arrest or, if the applicant has changed address, any new police station—and the justices' clerk or proper officer of the county court must deliver a copy of any new order to that station.

Role of the police

When an order exists which has a power of arrest attached to it, then a police constable can arrest the respondent if he or she has reasonable cause to suspect that the order has been breached. The respondent must be brought before the relevant court within 24 hours. Sundays and Bank Holidays do not count for this purpose. The relevant court is a court of the same tier as the court which made the order. In other words a family proceedings court can deal with the breach of a family proceedings court order, but a county court could not deal with a breach of such an order.

Options for the court following arrest

Following arrest, the court has two responsibilities and options:

- it can and ultimately must determine whether the facts and circumstances which led to the arrest amount to a breach of the order and if so what action if any to take. Thus, in practice, this option is normally only available at an immediate hearing if the respondent admits a breach or witnesses are available at short notice to give evidence. In some cases the arresting officer might be able to give such evidence. In other cases the evidence of the victim might be available. But even if evidence *is* available courts are unlikely to be willing to proceed without the respondent being legally represented; or

- it can adjourn the breach proceedings. The respondent may then be remanded (released) on bail or in custody until a future date.

Where bail is granted this is of the civil variety (i.e. not the same species of bail as in criminal proceedings, to which the Bail Act 1976 applies: *Chapter 2*). With civil bail, the arrested person will be required to enter into a recognizance (a promise to pay a sum of money fixed by the court to be enforced if the respondent does not attend court at the time and place fixed by the court) which he or she might then forfeit, at the behest of the court, if he or she does not attend court on the date of the future hearing. There is a prescribed form for this purpose, form FL410. The court may also require a surety (i.e. someone who is prepared to 'stand bail' by entering into a similar recognizance) to ensure that the respondent attends court. The prescribed form for this purpose is form FL411.

The arrested person must be dealt with within 14 days of being released (Sundays and Bank Holidays do not count) and must be given not less than two business days notice of the adjourned hearing.[1]

---

[1] Thus the court may not adjourn the hearing for less than two full days, *semble*.

However, these provisions do not stop the issue of a 'notice to show cause' for the same incident—an approach discussed below.

One further situation which should be mentioned is that where the respondent is released on bail but does not turn up at a hearing arranged within 14 days. *Wheeldon v Wheeldon* (1998) 1 FLR 463 appears to indicate that a respondent who had originally appeared following the exercise of a power of arrest can be re-arrested under the original power of arrest.

Written applications for bail

People arrested under a power of arrest (below) may apply for bail either orally or in writing. Written applications for bail are exceedingly rare in practice and there is no prescribed form, although in the county court form N244 is often used. A written application must contain the full name and address of the person making the application, the address where he or she is being detained, the address where he or she would reside if granted bail, the amount of any recognizance offered (see the explanations above), the grounds upon which the application is made and, where a previous application has been refused, full particulars of any change in circumstances since the refusal (rule 21 FPC rules; rule 3.10 FPR rules).

Any written application must be signed by the respondent or person acting on his or her behalf, i.e. their solicitor or by a *guardian ad litem* if the person making the application is a minor or incapable of acting for himself or herself. A copy must be served by the person making the application on the applicant under Part IV of the Family Law Act.

WHERE NO POWER OF ARREST IS ATTACHED

If the original order did not contain a power of arrest or if the respondent gave an undertaking to the court (*Chapter 4*), an application can be made for a warrant of arrest if it is alleged that an order or undertaking has been breached. The application may be made in form FL407 for the issue of a warrant of arrest and it must specify details of the breach and will be substantiated on oath.

In the family proceedings court, a single justice from the family panel can deal with the application. In the county court, a district judge will deal with it. If the warrant is granted it will be in form FL408. The warrant can be without bail or may be endorsed with provisions allowing bail and requiring the respondent to enter into a recognizance to ensure his or her attendance and if required to produce sureties. The justices' clerk or, in the county court, the proper officer, is responsible for delivery of the warrant issued in form FL408 to the police station for the area of the applicant's arrest. In the county court the warrant may be executed by bailiffs (rule 3.9A(3) FPR Rules).

Once the warrant has been executed, the procedure generally follows that described above in the case of an order with a power of arrest.

NOTICE TO SHOW CAUSE

This procedure applies more widely. If a respondent fails to comply with an order or undertaking the applicant can ask the justices' clerk or the proper officer of the county court, as appropriate, to issue a notice to show cause why the respondent should not be committed to custody. In the family proceedings court this is by way of form FL418; in the county court form N78 (under Order 29, County Court Rules 1981).[2]

The rules are sile nt as to whether applications can be oral or have to be in writing, but in his or her request the applicant must identify the provisions of the order alleged to have been breached and—even if an oral request is acceptable—support the allegations by a written statement the contents of which set out the grounds for making the application (i.e. the date, time, place and nature of the alleged breach) which he or she must sign and declare to be true. In the county court such a statement needs to be sworn.

This form and statement will normally be served on the respondent by the applicant unless the court decides to dispense with service if it thinks it just to do so. The court could come to this decision if, e.g. it believes service of a notice might result in the respondent engaging in acts of violence towards the applicant. The form recites the order and undertaking and the way in which it is alleged the order or undertaking has been breached and informs the respondent that the applicant has applied for an order that he or she should be committed to custody. It then gives a court date and requires the respondent to attend and show cause why he or she should not be dealt with in that way.

The right of the applicant to apply for such a notice to be issued appears to be available irrespective of whether a power of arrest (above) has been attached to the order. Such an application might be made if the applicant is not satisfied with the efforts of the police to arrest the respondent—and he or she may chose to expedite matters using this method. If an order exists without a power of arrest and the respondent is subject to an undertaking, then again the applicant may think this procedure quicker than applying for a warrant of arrest.

---

[2] In the family proceedings court the applicant's request replaces the need for a complaint (application) and a notice to show cause replaces the usual requirement for a summons to be served on the respondent before the court can exercise its powers under s.63(3) MCA 1980: see later in the chapter.

POWERS WHERE A BREACH IS PROVED

By whatever route the enforcement proceedings reach court, if the court finds the breach proved it must next decide what, if any, order if any to make. If the court considers that an order is necessary to deal with the breach it effectively has three alternatives:

- immediate committal to prison

- committal to prison suspended on such terms as it, the court, thinks fit

- a financial penalty

Alternatively, the court may conclude that the best way to deal with the case is to make 'no order'. All these options are discussed in the text below. The decision of the court must be recorded on form FL419 (form N79 in the county court). This form requires the court to give exact details of its decision, full details of the hearing and of the facts found by the court, etc.

If the decision is an immediate committal to prison, the warrant of committment will be completed in form FL420 (form N80 in the county court).

Form FL419 (form N79 in the county court) (both as mentioned above) must be served on the respondent at the same time as the execution of any warrant or within 36 hours.

Committal to prison

Detailed rules lay down the procedure which courts must follow before committing a respondent who is in breach of an order or undertaking to prison. These generally follow the County Court Rules which existed prior to the introduction of Part IV Family Law Act 1996. The magistrates' courts procedure has been brought into line so as to introduce the same safeguards that existed in the county court previously.

An order cannot generally be enforced by committal unless the respondent knew about it and personal service of a non-molestation order or occupation order is usually required before the court can proceed to committal (rule 20(6)(a) FPC rules; CCR Order 29, rule 1(2)(a) see further below). Furthermore an order requiring an act to be done cannot be enforced unless the order is served before the expiration of the period of time directed for this act to be accomplished (rule 20(6)(b) FPC rules; CCR Order 29, rule 1(2)(b)). However, where the order requires the respondent to abstain from any act—as orders often do—it may be enforced by committal even if not personally served provided that the court is satisfied that the respondent had notice of its terms—because present when the order was made or notified of its terms by telephone or otherwise (rule 20(11) FPC rules; CCR Order 29, rule 1(6)).

A non-molestation order will contain provisions prohibiting molestation. The justices' clerk or the proper officer of the county court is required to incorporate a notice as to the consequences of disobedience which should act as a warning to the respondent. Where the Part IV order is purely an occupation order, the justices' clerk or proper officer of the court is only obliged to incorporate such a notice if the court so directs (rule 20(7) FPC rules; CCR Order 29, rule 1(3) and see rule 3.9A(5) FPR). Good practice dictates that in most cases a similar notice should be incorporated into all orders routinely. Failure to do so could compromise the availability of swift enforcement action.

The court may dispense with service of the order or a notice to show cause if the court considers it just to do so (rule 20(12) FPC rules; CCR Order 29, rule 1(7)). This may be appropriate e.g. where the respondent has moved to an address which is not known to the applicant and is, in effect, untraceable. If the court dispenses with service or a notice to show cause and a committal order is made in the respondent's absence, the court may fix a date and time when the respondent is to be brought before the court to be given the opportunity to make representations (r.20(13) FP rules; CCR Order 29, r.1(8)).

Committal orders are made in form FL419 (in the county court form N79) and a warrant of committal in form FL420 (county court form N80).

Maximum periods and formalities

As already indicated above, the maximum period of imprisonment under s.63 Magistrates' Courts Act 1980 is two months. In the county court, under section 14(1) County Court Act 1984 the maximum period is two years. Unless the court orders otherwise, the committal order must be served on the respondent personally either before or at the time of the execution of the warrant (r.20(10) FP rules; CCR Order 29, rule 1(5)). In practice, it would appear that the police require a copy of the warrant and two copies of the committal order. One copy of the order is then served by them on the respondent when they execute the warrant.

Alternatives to committal

Before making an immediate committal order, the court has a duty to consider whether alternative means of disposal would be more appropriate. Accordingly, committal need not be immediate. The court has power by order to suspend execution of the warrant for such term and on such conditions as thinks fit/may specify (rule 20(16) FPC rules;

RSC Order 52, rule 7(1)). When the court suspends execution, the applicant must—unless the court otherwise directs—serve on the respondent a notice informing him or her of the terms of the suspension (rule 20(17) FPC rules; RSC Order 52, rule 7(2)). There is no requirement for service of such a notice to be effected personally.

The sanction in the county court is imprisonment of up to two years or an unlimited financial penalty. In the family proceedings court (or magistrates' court if being enforced there) section 63(3) Magistrates' Courts Act 1980 provides:

> where any person disobeys an order of a magistrates' court . . . to do anything other than the payment of money or to abstain from doing anything the court may:
> (a) order him to pay a sum not exceeding £50 for every day during which he is in default or a sum not exceeding £5000; or
> (b) commit him to custody until he has remedied his default or for a period not exceeding two months;
> but a person who is ordered to pay a sum for every day during which he is in default or is committed to custody until he has remedied his default shall not by virtue of this section be ordered to pay more than £1000 or be committed for more than two months in all for doing or abstaining from doing the same thing, contrary to the order.[3]

In the county court *only*, enforcement may be by possession vis-à-vis any exclusion requirement in an occupation order (CCR, Order 26, rule 17(2); form N235). A bailiff executes any such warrant.

General power to adjourn and make 'no order'

The court can adjourn consideration of any penalty for breach and the case may be restored if the respondent does not comply with any conditions imposed by the court (section 50 FLA 1996). This allows the court in appropriate cases to make 'no order' following proof of breach (at least *pro tem*). As already indicated, it is fairly common practice for judges to adjourn enforcement in this way, for a fixed period, provided no further breach occurs in the interim and any other conditions imposed by the court are met. If the tactic works, the case is marked 'no action taken on the breach': the initial appearance was warning enough.

Application to purge contempt

If the respondent is in custody by virtue of a warrant or an order and wishes to apply for it to be discharged, he or she may make an

---

[3] The Children Act Advisory Committee has expressed the view that section 63(3) cannot apply to non-compliance with directions given by a justices' clerk or a single magistrate as the provision only applies to orders of *a court*.

application in writing witnessed by the prison governor showing that he or she has purged his or her contempt or wishes to do so. He or she must provide the other party (i.e. the applicant for the order or warrant) with at least one day's notice of making such an application (rule 20(15) FPC rules). It should also be noted that if someone is committed to prison in their absence the court may fix a time within which he or she must be returned to court (rule 20(13) FPC rules; CCR Order 29, rule 1(8)).

ENFORCEMENT OF UNDERTAKINGS

The provisions discussed above relating to notices to show cause (and the operation of a penal notice: see the example at p.63) also apply to the enforcement of undertakings—and the same procedures must be followed if, as a result of breach, a committal order is made. However, it should be noted that there is *no* authority or legal provision dispensing with service of an undertaking.

An undertaking must be recorded in form FL422 and must be delivered by the justices' clerk or in the county court by the proper officer of the court to the party giving the undertaking by either handing him or her a copy before he or she leaves the court building or by posting it to him or her, to his or her place of residence where known, or through his or her solicitor. If it is not possible to serve by one of these methods, the court must deliver a copy to the party for whose benefit the undertaking is given and require that party to serve it on the other party personally as soon as practicable.

NATURE OF CIVIL CUSTODY

The term *civil prisoner* describes someone who is in prison for a civil wrong rather than a criminal offence—such as contempt, failure to comply with a financial order, or e.g. a non-molestation order—*and for no other reason*. Rules about the treatment of civil prisoners are set out in HM Prison Service Standing Order 12. Civil prisoners will usually be in the company of other civil prisoners and are not required to associate with any other class of prisoner unless they agree and the governor approves this. In practice, shortage of accommodation may mean that they are placed where there is space. They can object, but 'standing on the rules' in prison often results in a harsher regime being experienced.

As with unconvicted prisoners charged with a criminal offence, civil prisoners have additional rights and facilities in line with those of remand prisoners awaiting trial. HM Prison Service has developed a Statement of Principle on how such prisoners should be treated and under which, so far as is consistent with the fact of imprisonment and security, they enjoy certain privileges—and the aim is to treat them in accordance with the *Citizen's Charter*.[4]

HOSPITAL AND GUARDIANSHIP ORDERS

Another alternative to a committal order is for the court to make a hospital order or guardianship order provided that certain criteria set out in the Mental Health Act 1983 apply. If such an order is made the court sends prescribed information which will be of assistance to the hospital in dealing with the patient and must inform the applicant when the respondent is transferred. As indicated in *Chapter 2*, this is a specialist area outside the scope of this work and readers are referred to publications dealing specifically with provisions about mental health.

POWER TO SET ASIDE AN ORDER

When an order has been made and it subsequently appears that the respondent had no knowledge of the application, the court may set aside

Materials: Chapter 6

KEY EXTRACTS FROM RULES OF PROCEDURE

Magistrates' Courts
The Family Proceedings Courts (Matrimonial Proceedings etc.) (Rules) 1991[5]

Enforcement of orders made on applications under Part IV of the Family Law Act 1996

20.—(1) Where a power of arrest is attached to one or more of the provisions ('the relevant provisions') of an order made under Part IV of the Family Law Act 1996
-

---

[4] This section is based on a passage in *The Prisons Handbook*, Mark Leech, Waterside Press (published annually) which contains some further details

[5] SI 1395/1991 as amended—including by the Family Proceedings Courts (Matrimonial Proceedings etc.) (Amendment) Rules 1997: effective 1 October 1997

(a) the relevant provisions shall be set out in Form FL406 and the form shall not include any provisions of the order to which the power of arrest was not attached; and

(b) a copy of the form shall be delivered to the officer for the time being in charge of any police station for the applicant's address or of such other police station as the court may specify.

The copy of the form delivered under sub-paragraph (b) shall be accompanied by a statement showing that the respondent has been served with the order or informed of its terms (whether by being present when the order was made or by telephone or otherwise).

(2) Where an order is made varying or discharging the relevant provisions, the justice's clerk shall -

(a) immediately inform the officer who received a copy of the form under paragraph (1) and, if the applicant's address has changed, the officer for the time being in charge of the police station for the new address; and

(b) deliver a copy of the order to any officer so informed.

(3) An application for the issue of a warrant for the arrest of the respondent shall be made in form FL407 and the warrant shall be issued in Form FL408 and delivered by the justice's clerk to the officer for the time being in charge of any police station for the respondent's address or of such other police station as the court may specify.

(4) The court before whom a person is brought following his arrest may -

(a) determine whether the facts, and the circumstances which led to the arrest, amounted to disobedience of the order, or

(b) adjourn the proceedings and, where such an order is made, the arrested person may be released and

(i) be dealt with within 14 days of the day on which he was arrested; and

(ii) be given not less than 2 business days' notice of the adjourned hearing.

Nothing in this paragraph shall prevent the issue of a notice under paragraph (8) if the arrested person is not dealt with within the period mentioned in sub-paragraph (b)(i) above.

(5) Paragraphs (6) to (13) shall apply for the enforcement of orders made on applications under Part IV of the Family Law Act 1996 by committal order.

(6) Subject to paragraphs (11) and (12), an order shall not be enforced by committal order unless -

(a) a copy of the order in Form FL404 has been served personally on the respondent; and

(b) where the order requires the respondent to do an act, the copy has been so served before the expiration of the time within which he was required to do the act and was accompanied by a copy of any order, made between the date of the order and the date of service, fixing that time.

(7) At the time when the order is drawn up, the justices' clerk shall-

(a) where the order made is (or includes) a non-molestation order, and

(b) where the order made is an occupation order and the court so directs, issue a copy of the order, indorsed with or incorporating a notice as to the consequences of disobedience, for service in accordance with paragraph (6).

(8) If the respondent fails to obey the order, the justices' clerk shall, at the request of the applicant, issue a notice in Form FL418 warning the respondent that an application will be made for him to be committed and, subject to paragraph (12), the notice shall be served on him personally.

(9) The request for issue of the notice under paragraph (8) shall be treated as a complaint and shall -

(a) identify the provisions of the order or undertaking which it is alleged have been disobeyed or broken;

(b) list the ways in which it is alleged that the order or undertaking has been disobeyed or broken;

(c) be supported by a statement which is signed and is declared to be true and which states the grounds on which the application is made,

and, unless service is dispensed with under paragraph (12), a copy of the statement shall be served with the notice.

(10) If an order in Form FL419 (a committal order) is made, it shall include provision for the issue of a warrant of committal in Form FL 420 and, unless the court otherwise orders -

(a) a copy of the order shall be served personally on the person to be committed either before or at the time of the execution of the warrant; or

(b) the order for the issue of the warrant may be served on the person to be committed at any time within 36 hours after the execution of the warrant.

(11) An order requiring a person to abstain from doing an act may be enforced by committal order notwithstanding that a copy of the order has not been served personally if the court is satisfied that, pending such service, the respondent had notice thereof either -

(a) by being present when the order was made;

(b) by being notified of the terms of the order whether by telephone or otherwise.

(12) The court may dispense with service of a copy of the order under paragraph (6) or a notice under paragraph (8) if the court thinks it just to do so.

(13) Where service of a notice to show cause is dispensed with under paragraph (12) and a committal order is made, the court may of its own motion fix a date and time when the person to be committed is to be brought before the court.

(14) Paragraphs (6) to (10), (12) and (13) shall apply to the enforcement of undertakings with the necessary modifications and as if

(a) for paragraph (6) there were substituted the following -

'(6) A copy of Form FL422 recording the undertaking shall be delivered by the justices' clerk to the party giving the undertaking

(a) by handing a copy of the document to him before he leaves the court building; or

(b) where his place of residence is known, by posting a copy to him at his place of residence; or

(c) through his solicitor,

and, where delivery cannot be effected in this way, the justices' clerk shall deliver a copy of the document to the party for whose benefit the undertaking is given and that party shall cause it to be served personally as soon as is practicable';

(b) in paragraph (12), the words from 'a copy' to 'paragraph (6) or' were omitted.

(15) Where a person in custody under a warrant or order, desires to apply to the court for his discharge, he shall make his application in writing attested by the governor of the prison showing that he has purged or is desirous of purging his contempt and the justices' clerk shall not less than one day before the application is heard, serve notice of it on the party (if any) at whose instance the warrant or order was issued.

(16) The court by whom an order of committal is made may by order direct that the execution of the order of committal shall be suspended for such period or on such terms or conditions as it may specify .

(17) Where execution of an order of committal is suspended by an order under paragraph (16), the applicant for the order of committal must, unless the court otherwise directs, serve on the person against whom it was made a notice informing him of the making and terms of the order under that paragraph.

(18) The court may adjourn consideration of the penalty to be imposed for contempts found proved and such consideration may be restored if the respondent does not comply with any conditions specified by the court.

(19) Where the court makes a hospital order in Form FL413 or a guardianship order in Form FL414 under the Mental Health Act 1983, the justices' clerk shall -

(a) send to the hospital any information which will be of assistance in dealing with the patient;

(b) inform the applicant when the respondent is being transferred to hospital.

(20) Where a transfer direction given by the Secretary of State under section 48 of the Mental Health Act 1983 is in force in respect of a person remanded in custody by the court, the justices' clerk shall notify -

(a) the governor of the prison to which that person was remanded; and

(b) the hospital where he is detained,

of any committal hearing which that person is required to attend and the justices' clerk shall give notice in writing to the hospital where that person is detained of any further remand.

(21) An order for the remand of the respondent shall be in Form FL409 and an order discharging the respondent from custody shall be in Form FL421.

(22) In paragraph (4) 'arrest' means arrest under a power of arrest attached to an order or under a warrant of arrest.

Applications under Part IV of the Family Law Act 1996: bail

21. — (1) An application for bail made by a person arrested under a power of arrest may be made either orally or in writing.

(2) Where an application is made in writing, it shall contain the following particulars -

(a) the full name of the person making the application;

(b) the address of the place where the person making the application is detained at the time that the application is made;

(c) the address where the person making the application would reside if he were to be granted bail;

(d) the amount of the recognizance in which he would agree to be bound; and

(e) the grounds on which the application is made and, where a previous application has been refused, full particulars of any change in circumstances which has occured since the refusal.

(3) An application made in writing shall be signed by the person making the application or a person duly authorised by him in that behalf or, where the person making the application is for any reason incapable of acting, by a guardian ad litem acting on his behalf and a copy shall be served by the making the application on the applicant for the Part IV order.

(4) The following forms shall be used:

(a) the recognizance of the person making the application shall be in Form FL410 and that of a surety in Form FL411;

(b) a bail notice in Form FL412 shall be given to the respondent where he is remanded on bail.

County Courts

County Courts
Family Proceedings
Supreme Court of England and Wales

The Family Proceedings Rules 1991 [6]

Enforcement of orders made on applications under Part IV of the Family Law Act 1996

3.9A – (1) Where a power of arrest is attached to one or more of the provisions ('the relevant provisions') of an order made under Part IV of the Family Law Act 1996 -

(a) the relevant provisions shall be set out in Form FL406 and the form shall not include any provisions of the order to which the power of arrest was not attached; and

(b) a copy of the form shall be delivered to the officer for the time being in charge of any police station for the applicant's address or of such other police station as the court may specify.

The copy of the form delivered under sub-paragraph (b) shall be accompanied by a statement showing that the respondent has been served with the order or informed of its terms (whether by being present when the order was made or by telephone or otherwise).

(2) Where an order is made varying or discharging the relevant provisions, the proper officer shall -

(a) immediately inform the officer who received a copy of the form under paragraph (1) and, if the applicant's address has changed, the officer for the time being in charge of the police station for the new address; and

(b) deliver a copy of the order to any officer so informed.

---

[6] Key amendments effected by the the Family Proceedings (Amendment No.3) Rules 1997 (SI 1893/1997)

(3) An application for the issue of a warrant for the arrest of the respondent shall be made in Form FL407 and the warrant shall be issued in Form FL408.

(4) The court before whom a person is brought following his arrest may -

  (a) determine whether the facts, and the circumstances which led to the arrest, amounted to disobedience of the order, or

  (b) adjourn the proceedings and, where such an order is made, the arrested person may be released and

   (i) be dealt with within 14 days of the day on which he was arrested; and

   (ii) be given not less than 2 days' notice of the adjourned hearing.

Nothing in this paragraph shall prevent the issue of a notice under CCR Order 29, rule 1(4) if the arrested person is not dealt with within the period mentioned in sub-paragraph (b)(i) above.

(5) The following provisions shall apply, with the necessary modifications, to the enforcement of orders made on applications under Part IV of the Family Law Act 1996 -

  (a) RSC Order 52, rule 7 (power to suspend execution of committal order);

  (b) (in a case where an application for an order of committal is made to the High Court) RSC Order 52, rule 2 (application for leave);(c) CCR Order 29, rule 1 (committal for breach of order);

  (d) CCR Order 29, rule 1A (undertakings);

  (e) CCR Order 29, rule 3 (discharge of person in custody); and CCR Order 29, rule 1 shall have effect, as if for paragraph (3), there were substituted the following -

   '(3) At the time when the order is drawn up, the proper officer shall-

   (a) where the order made is (or includes) a non-molestation order and

   (b) where the order made is an occupation order and the court so directs, issue a copy of the order, indorsed with or incorporating a notice as to the consequences of disobedience, for service in accordance with paragraph (2).'.

(6) The court may adjourn consideration of the penalty to be imposed for contempts found proved and such consideration may be restored if the respondent does not comply with any conditions specified by the court.

(7) Where the court makes a hospital order in Form FL413 or a guardianship order in Form FL414 under the Mental Health Act 1983, the proper officer shall

  (a) send to the hospital any information which will be of assistance in dealing with the patient;

  (b) inform the applicant when the respondent is being transferred to hospital.

(8) Where a transfer direction given by the Secretary of State under section 48 of the Mental Health Act 1983 is in force in respect of a person remanded in custody by the court under Schedule 5 to the Family Law Act 1996, the proper officer shall notify

  (a) the governor of the prison to which that person was remanded; and

  (b) the hospital where he is detained, of any committal hearing which that person is required to attend and the proper officer shall give notice in writing to the hospital where that person is detained of any further remand under paragraph 3 of Schedule 5 to the Family Law Act 1996.

(9) An order for the remand of the respondent shall be in Form FL409.

(10) In paragraph (4) 'arrest' means arrest under a power of arrest attached to an order or under a warrant of arrest.

Applications under Part IV of the Family Law Act 1996: bail

3.10—(1) An application for bail made by a person arrested under a power of arrest or a warrant of arrest may be made either orally or in writing.

(2) Where an application is made in writing, it shall contain the following particulars

(a) the full name of the person making the application;

(b) the address of the place where the person making the application is detained at the time when the application is made;

(c) the address where the person making the application would reside if he were to be granted bail;

(d) the amount of the recognizance in which he would agree to be bound; and

(e) the grounds on which the application is made and, where a previous application has been refused, full particulars of any change in circumstances which has occurred since that refusal.

(3) An application made in writing shall be signed by the person making the application or by a person duly authorised by him in that behalf or, where the person making the application is a minor or is for any reason incapable of acting, by a guardian ad litem acting on his behalf and a copy shall be served by the person making the application on the applicant for the Part IV order.

(4) The persons prescribed for the purposes of paragraph 4 of Schedule 5 to the Family Law Act 1996 (postponement of taking of recognizance) are

(a) a district judge,

(b) a justice of the peace,

(c) a justices' clerk,

(d) a police officer of the rank of inspector or above or in charge of a police station, and

(e) (where the person making the application is in his custody) the governor or keeper of a prison.

(5) The person having custody of the person making the application shall -

(a) on receipt of a certificate signed by or on behalf of the district judge stating that the recognizance of any sureties required have been taken, or on being otherwise satisfied that all such recognizances have been taken; and

(b) on being satisfied that the person making the application has entered into his recognizance, release the person making the application.

(6) The following forms shall be used:

(a) the recognizance of the person making the application shall be in Form FL410 and that of a surety in Form FL411;

(b) a bail notice in Form FL412 shall be given to the respondent where he is remanded on bail.

CHAPTER 7

Protection from Harassment

An understanding of the remedies available to survivors and potential victims of domestic violence would be incomplete without an outline of relatively new-style provisions affecting individuals who are subjected to personal interference in the form of harassment. These remedies are not confined to domestic violence or family situations, but have become a valuable tool in this context.

PROTECTION FROM HARASSMENT ACT 1997

The 1997 Act came into force in June 1997 (with the exception of sub-sections 3(6) to (9) which are still not in force at the time of writing: see *Forthcoming civil remedy*, p.145). Unlike the long-debated Family Law Act 1996, the 1997 Act passed through Parliament in just over three months. This was due mainly to concern about 'stalking'—paying unsolicited attention to someone by following, watching or pestering them. Notoriously, some public figures suffered in this way, drawing attention to the inadequacy of the then law—and in other well-publicised cases such behaviour turned into something altogether more serious. The National Anti-Stalking and Harassment Campaign (NASH) and similar organizations urged that the law be changed; and the main political parties elevated law and order on their agendas as the general election of 1997 approached—which undoubtedly influenced matters.

The long title of the 1997 Act describes it as 'An Act to make provision for protecting persons from harassment and similar conduct'. To this end the Act introduced:

- two new *criminal* offences
  — harassment (section 2)
  — putting people in fear of violence (section 4)

- the 'restraining order': an entirely new sentencing power. The restraining order can be made by criminal courts ancillary to an appropriate sentence following conviction for either of the above offences (section 5)

- a new *civil* remedy (in effect the *statutory* tort of harassment) (section 3) together with

— a specific statutory power for civil courts to make an injunction prohibiting further harassment (*ibid*)

— a right to apply for someone subject to such an 'anti-harassment' injunction to be arrested (*ibid*)

— a further new *criminal* offence of doing anything prohibited by an anti-harassment injunction. This unique 'cross-over' arrangement whereby breach of an order made in a civil court is punishable as an offence in a criminal court is provided for in section 3(6) and (9) *when in force*

• a common test for harassment in both criminal proceedings under section 2 and civil proceedings under section 3.

Victims of harassment thus now have a clear choice as to which court to seek a remedy in.

As already indicated, the 1997 Act is in force apart from sub-sections 3(6) to (9). No special procedural rules exist in relation the Act it at time of writing (the statute making no provision for this).

A NOTE ABOUT THE PRE-EXISTING LAW

The pre-existing law is instructive and assists understanding.

Civil law

Earlier developments are especially relevant in relation to civil proceedings where existing case law is likely to influence the approach of the High Court and county court. Until *Burris v. Adzani* [1995] 4 All ER 802[1] no tort dealt directly with harassment. That case, and particularly the leading judgement of Sir Thomas Bingham (then Master of the Rolls), clarified that there was a specific, primary tort of 'harassment' and the Court of Appeal laid down principles to be applied by courts dealing with applications for related injunctions. These principles are likely to be influential when dealing with applications under section 3 and are discussed later in this chapter. Certain difficulties persisted under the former law however: there was no jurisdiction to attach a power of arrest to an injunction granted to prevent harassment; and the procedure which did exist of applying for a respondent to be dealt with for contempt of

---

[1] It is arguable that the common law tort survives the 1997 Act and runs in tandem with it. If so, it is not tied to the statutory criteria, of course. Equally, other cases have eqivocated concerning the existence of a specific common law tort of harassment: see *Khorasandjian v Bush* [1193] QB 727; *Hunter v Canary Wharf Ltd.* [1997] AC 655.

court was cumbersome. Section 3 of the 1997 Act addresses some of these points (when fully in force).

Criminal law

A variety of—sometimes quite serious—criminal offences may be committed within a domestic violence context (see, generally, *Chapter 2*). Examples most akin to forms of harassment include:

- causing fear or provoking violence by using threatening, abusive or insulting words or behaviour contrary to section 4 Public Order Act 1986. Interestingly, a new section 4A of the 1986 Act was inserted by section 154 Criminal Justice and Public Order Act 1994 so as to create an offence of 'intentional harassment'. However, this provision does not appear to have been widely used, possibly because the prosecutor must establish a *subjective* intention on the part of the accused. Someone might act irrationally—perhaps because he or she is infatuated, or sees himself or herself as in the right, or as being the 'victim' of events within a relationship—but may not *intend* to harass.

- causing harassment alarm or distress by using threatening, abusive or insulting words or behaviour, or disorderly behaviour, contrary to section 5 Public Order Act 1996

- making malicious telephone calls contrary to section 43 Telecommunications Act 1994

- sending malicious letters through the post contrary to section 1 Malicious Communications Act 1988

- where actual violence is used or attempted, or there are threats to kill, or sexual connotations, various offences may be committed under the Offences Against the Person Act 1861 or a number of Sexual Offences Acts (or Amendment Acts) from 1956 onwards.

Widening of the law of assault
In *R v Burstow* (*The Times*, 30 July 1996) the Court of Appeal extended the general law of assault in ways relevant to harassment. Three new principles were laid down, viz:

- an assault can occur without the use of direct physical force
- grievous bodily harm includes physiological injury; and
- a campaign of non-physical harassment which causes physiological harm can constitute physiological assault.

In *R v Ireland* (*The Times*, 22 May 1996)[2] three principles were laid down in connection with communications, namely:

- a telephone call (or series of calls) can constitute assault

- to do so, such calls must place victims in immediate fear for their safety with resulting physiological injury. Merely causing fear, distress or pain is insufficient

- in order to establish assault, physiological injury resulting from the telephone call must be established.

Seemingly, the principles in *R v Ireland* would extend to other forms of modern communication: E-mail, across the Internet, or (on the horizon) via digital TV. However, although the above developments may widen the protection of the criminal law, the criteria are quite narrow and any idea that they provide a proper remedy for harassment was dented by several high profile acquittals. One of the most significant occurred in 1996 when a man was found not guilty of behaviour likely to cause a breach of the peace after he tried to break through a security cordon protecting HRH The Princess Royal. 'Peaceful' behaviour did not constitute an offence, however unacceptable.[3]

PROTECTION FROM HARASSMENT ACT 1997

Section 1 of the 1997 Act prohibits a course of conduct which amounts to harassment. Anyone who breaches this prohibition may be subject to criminal or civil proceedings as described later in this chapter.

The common statutory test for harassment
Section 1 of the 1997 Act provides:

(1) A person must not pursue a course of conduct—
   (a) which amounts to harassment of another, and
   (b) which he knows or ought to know amounts to harassment of the other.

---

[2] See also *R v Constanza* [1997] 2 Cr. App. R 492

[3] It can be noted that this defendant was not required to enter into a recognizance, i.e. be bound over to keep the peace and be of good behaviour pursuant to the Justices of the Peace Act 1361, a power available whether a defendant is convicted or not: *Chapter 2*. Indeed, 'inoffensive' behaviour is not enough for a bind over (*Redmond-Bate v Director of Public Prosecutions* (1999), *The Times*, July 28, whereas it might be for harassmnent—provided the victim is affected and the perpetrator knows that he or she will be.

(2) For the purposes of this section, the person whose course of conduct is in question ought to know that it amounts to harassment of another if a reasonable person in possession of the same information would think the course of conduct amounted to harassment of the other.

Thus section 1(2)(b) introduces both *subjective* and *objective* tests of *mens rea*: see further under *Mental element*, below.

Although stalking may have been the *raison d'être* for the Act—and *is* addressed—the prohibition is potentially wide-ranging. It would, for instance, cover harassment in a variety of situations: domestic, work, sexual, neighbour disputes, racial taunts, and unwelcome attention generally. The key ingredients of the prohibition in section 1 are:

Harassment
The course of conduct must amount to 'harassment'. This is not defined in the 1997 Act (nor 'molestation' in the Family Law Act 1996: *Chapter 3*) and is thus a matter for the court on the facts and in the circumstances of individual cases. However, section 7(2) states that references 'to harassing a person *include* alarming the person or causing the person distress' (emphasis added). Dictionary definitions of harassment use words such as 'annoy', 'aggravate', 'bother', 'hound', 'molest', 'persecute', 'pester', 'plague', 'torment', 'worry', 'cause nuisance' and 'wear out'. It is thus possible to envisage harassment covering a wide range of behaviour, the circumstances in which alarm or distress etc. can be caused in the context, say, of a one-time relationship which has ended being virtually unlimited. Typical behaviour (if there is such a thing) in a domestic context might include disrupting the victims life, wearing her down by one means or another, playing on known dislikes, distastes or pre-occupations, causing general discomfort or mayhem by visits or telephone calls, or making demands and seeking to control events by intimidating behaviour, threats or innuendo.

The use in section 1(1)(b) of the words 'which he knows . . . amount to harassment' seem to place the outer limits of harassment within a myriad of potential sensitivities on the part of a victim—provided that the perpetrator has actual knowledge that certain (possibly quite ordinary, everyday) actions happen to cause alarm and distress, etc to the victim: see further under *Mental element*, below.[4]

---

[4] Some corroboration for this view can be found in *Harassment Law and Practice*, Addison N and Lawson-Cruttenden T, Blackstone Press, 1998; and see 'What is Harassment', Leonard Jason-Lloyd, 163 JPN 604. The government declined to limit or further define harassment, preferring to leave its scope to the courts. But quare whether the resulting 'uncertainty' can survive the impact of the Human Rights Act 1997. Readers are also referred to footnote 14 on page 151.

The course of conduct

Whether or not incidents amount to a course of conduct is again for the court to decide in an individual case. However, section 7(3) stipulates that a course of conduct must involve conduct on *at least two occasions*.[5] Conduct can include speech: section 7(4).

There is no requirement for the incidents in the course of conduct to be of the same type. Breaking a window on Tuesday followed by a telephone call deliberately causing annoyance on Thursday could thus be caught by the provisions in appropriate circumstances. Factors such as a lapse of time between incidents may be relevant. The interval might be too short for a court to treat incidents as separate items in a course of conduct—certainly if the gap is very short—rather than as all part of a single incident, e.g. if someone causes interference at 11.10 p.m. and then repeats this a minute later. It may be correspondingly difficult to make a factual assessment where the incidents are months or years apart. However behaviour occurring, say, on the anniversary of the termination of a relationship, if it happened consistently, or at least twice (section 7(3)), could, it seems, constitute a course of conduct notwithstanding the lapse of time between incidents. (With longer gaps there may be a problem with regard to time limits so far as summary criminal offences are concerned: below). It is possible that there will need to be some kind of nexus or continuum from which it can be inferred that there is, indeed, a *course* of conduct as opposed to totally separate, isolated and unconnected events. But the greater the number of incidents the less the scope for innocent explanation or claims of coincidence it seems.

The presumption against retroactive legislation suggests that any course of conduct must have started on or after 16 June 1997 (when the 1997 Act came into force), with at least two incidents occurring after that date. Also, section 2 creates a *purely summary* offence so that any criminal proceedings under that section must take place within six months of the act or events in question: section 127 Magistrates' Courts Act 1980 (contrast the position in relation to the more serious offence under section 4 below, which is not affected by statutory time constraints).[6]

---

[5] If the common law tort has survived the 1997 Act (footnote 1) it is not restricted to 'a course of conduct'. Arguably, unconnected events or a one-off occurence which is sufficiently illustrative of harassment would suffice—as it might to show that the statutory tort has been committed via 'apprehension' of a course of conduct as oppposed to an actual breach of section 1: see p.144

[6] The authors have encountered the view that provided at least one incident has taken place within six months of the commencement of summary proceedings reference could be made to incidents which occurred more than six months ago. Ultimately, this point, not anticipated by the Parliamentary draftsmen, can only be resolved on appeal.

It should be emphasised that each incident needs to be established to the required standard before a court can take it into account and according to whether the case is a civil or a criminal one. Readers are also referred to the section headed *Admissibility of Earlier Incidents,* towards the end of this chapter.

Mental element

As indicated above, in adopting the formula 'which the defendant *knows* or *ought to know* amounts to harassment' (emphasis added), section 1 lays down *subjective* and *objective* tests in the alternative. The latter is reinforced by section 1(2)(b) which states that a defendant ought to know that his or her course of conduct amounts to harassment 'if a reasonable person in possession of the same information would think the course of conduct amounted to harassment'. It may sometimes be obvious what any reasonable person would think about the events, but it may be less clear if, e.g. the victim was unduly sensitive or over-reacted to what appeared to be normal or everyday behaviour. In this context, it cannot be over emphasised that the reasonableness test in section 1(2) only comes into play under the objective ('ought to have known') limb of section 1(1)(b).

It might be advisable for a victim/survivor of 'subjective harassment' (i.e. where the allegation is that the perpetrator 'knows' it is having the effect of harassing him or her) to state this fact to the alleged perpetrator saying what impact the relevant behaviour is having—in express terms and possibly by solicitor's letter. Any repetition of it would then be accompanied by potential evidence of the requisite knowledge.[7] Failing this, the notice could support an inference that reasonable people would thereafter have concluded that the conduct amounted to harassment. Obviously, the behaviour would still have to fit the definition of harassment, but as we have already pointed out that definition is so wide and vague as to permit almost total flexibility if a subjective test of knowledge is relied upon (see p.134). As Leonard Jason-Lloyd points out at 163 JPN 607 the eggshell skull principle should not be overlooked—where the defendant takes the victim as he finds her and '. . . in *Malcolm v Broadhurst* [1970] 3 All ER 508 [a civil case but the point is equally applicable here] it was established that there is no difference between an eggshell skull and an eggshell personality'. He also makes the valid point that from the point of view of both the 1997 Act and other statutes which have used the word harassment without defining it, harassment 'seems to be judged as much by its effect on the victim as its causes'.

---

[7] Arguably, there might be a need for at least two incidents *after* the warning to constitute a course of conduct.

Where must the events occur?

The Act is silent as to whether all events must occur within the normal jurisdiction of the courts in England and Wales. It can be suggested that a course of conduct pursued wholly or partly from abroad, e.g. by telephone would be actionable in England and Wales assuming that the *effects* of the harassment took place here and the alleged perpetrator returned to that jurisdiction.

CRIMINAL OFFENCES UNDER SECTIONS 2 & 4

The 1997 Act creates two offences, of different levels of seriousness.

Section 2

Section 2 renders someone who contravenes section 1 guilty of an offence. Action will normally occur by way of police investigation and charge and subsequent review by a Crown prosecutor. However, due to the nature of the subject matter, there could be a significant number of private prosecutions (*Chapter 2*). Section 2 simply provides that:

(1) A person who pursues a course of conduct under section 1 is guilty of an offence.

The offence under section 2 is triable summarily and carries a maximum penalty of six months' imprisonment or a level 5 fine (£5000), or both: section 1(2)—as well as the other sentencing options which are available when someone is convicted of such a criminal offence, i.e. discharges, community sentence or a hospital order or guardianship if appropriate. Similarly, the standard magistrates' court powers to award compensation for injury, loss or damage apply, i.e. of up to £5,000 per offence: section 35 Powers of Criminal Courts Act 1973. There is, in effect, a presumption that compensation should be awarded where the court has power to do so, i.e. where loss, damage or injury has resulted from the offence: see, generally, *Chapter 2*.

In addition to the standard penalties and order—and unique to harassment—a restraining order can be made under section 5 of the 1997 Act: see *Restraining Orders* later in this chapter. The offence is an arrestable offence within the meaning of section 24(2) Police and Criminal Evidence Act 1984 (section 2(3) of the 1997 Act) meaning that the police can arrest without a warrant if they have reasonable grounds for believing that the offence has been committed.

Relationship between section 2 offences and other criminal offences

Sometimes incidents in a course of conduct may be criminal offences in their own right. For example, if an ex-partner on separate evenings shouts obscenities in the direction of the house where his or her former partner lives, each of these incidents could amount to an offence under section 5 Public Order Act 1986, whereas the whole events could also be a course of conduct under section 1. Whether the perpetrator could be dealt with in summary proceedings for any public order offences plus an offence under section 1 of the 1997 Act depends upon how the rule against double jeopardy applies to the facts of the particular case. Under that rule, sometimes known as the *nemo bis punire* rule, a defendant cannot be punished twice for the self-same matter, i.e. upon the exact same facts. The law here is complex and further discussion is outside the scope of a this book. Details should be sought in specialist works on magistrates' court procedure.[8]

Section 4

Section 4 of the 1997 Act creates a separate and intrinsically more serious offence of 'putting a person in fear of violence', i.e. a completely free-standing offence with different criteria as opposed to an aggravated version of that under section 2 above). Neither does the offence under section 4 rely on the common prohibition in section 1. The definition of 'course of conduct' *is* the same, but the *type of conduct* in question is more serious. Section 4 provides that:

(1) A person whose course of conduct causes another to fear, on at least two occasions, that violence will be used against him is guilty of an offence if he knows or ought to know that his course of conduct will cause the other so to fear on each of those occasions.

(2) For the purposes of this section, the person whose course of conduct is in question ought to know that it will cause another to fear that violence will be used against him on any occasion if a reasonable person in possession of the same information would cause the other so to fear on that occasion.

This is an either way offence. It carries a maximum penalty on indictment of five years' imprisonment or an unlimited fine, or both; and on summary conviction of six months' imprisonment or a fine not

---

[8] In practice, when a prosecutor decides to make overlapping allegations the most likely course is that the court will ask him or her to elect at the outset on which charge or charges he or she wishes to proceed, and to deal with other matters by adjourning them *sine die* (indefinitely). The *nemo bis punire* rule would then come into play if the defendant stood convicted and sentenced on the first matter and the prosecutor sought to reintroduce and prosecute a matter held in abeyance.

exceeding the statutory maximum (£5,000), or both. As with a conviction under section 2, other sentences are available and a restraining order can be made: see *Restraining Orders,* below. The normal powers and principles of compensation for injury, loss or damage apply. Compensation is unlimited in the Crown Court; and up to £5,000 per offence may be awarded in the magistrates' court. The six months' time limit for summary offences (p.135) does not apply to either way matters.

Ingredients of a section 4 offence

Certain comments made earlier in this chapter apply equally to section 2 and section 4 offences, whilst other ingredients are unique to section 4.

The course of conduct

Section 4(1) requires there to have been a 'course of conduct'. Whilst the meaning of this phrase is governed by the same considerations that we have already looked at in relation to section 2—*at least two incidents* are required (section 7(3)); these may include speech (section 7(4))—section 4 requires that 'on both or at least two occasions' the conduct caused another person to fear that violence would be used against him or her. Thus fear must have been caused on a minimum of two occasions and there must have been a minimum of two incidents.[9]

Mental element

As with section 2 offences, a *subjective* or *objective* test of *mens rea* applies in the alternative (see the general comments about this aspect of section 2 above). However, with section 4, what the defendant must be shown to have *known* or what he or she *ought to have known* is greatly enhanced in relation to each incident, i.e. 'that it will cause another to fear that violence will be used against him on any occasion': section 4(1), (2).

Alternative verdicts

If an accused person is tried in the Crown Court and found not guilty of a section 4 offence the jury may find him or her guilty of the lesser

---

[9] It is tempting to point to a certain lack of logic here, since any incidents over and above those involving fear, provided there are at least two of these, but which do not themselves involve fear, are *ex hypothesi* superfluous so far as the ingredients of section 4 are concerned. However, the existence of extra incidents which do not involve fear may serve to reinforce the inference that there was a *course of conduct* in relation to those incidents where fear *was* present. The curious way in which the provision is drafted may also have something to do with the alternative verdict provisions, when a jury in the Crown Court may often be faced with deciding whether (a) there was a course of conduct; and then (b) whether at least two incidents involved fear.

offence under section 2. The judge then has the same powers as if the defendant had been convicted in the magistrates' court of a section 2 offence. But where the case is tried in the magistrates' court the alternative verdict provisions *do not apply*, so that in a case where the prosecutor senses that there is arguably sufficient evidence for a section 4 conviction, but alive to the possibility of acquittal, he or she can make appropriate representations at the mode of trial/venue before plea stage, i.e. to the effect that the case should, perhaps, be committed to the Crown Court for trial.

Comparison with other offences

How does a section 4 offence sit alongside other offences? While, strictly speaking, many cases which fall within the ambit of section 4 could be dealt with summarily under section 2 (and without the need to prove fear etc.)—and especially as a restraining order can be added to any sentence—seriously threatening, aggressive or repetitive behaviour which meets the demands of section 4 will no doubt compel the police (or the survivor) to consider proceedings under this section. Analogous conduct is proscribed by the Public Order Act 1986 and without the need for two or more incidents—but those offences do not attract the novel power handed to courts by the 1997 Act to make a restraining order. As compared with the law of assault, section 4 can be used without having to wait until actual physical or physiological harm occurs or is attempted.

RESTRAINING ORDERS

On conviction under section 2 or section 4, a restraining order can be made. It should be emphasised yet again that there is *no power* to make a restraining order when someone is convicted of any other criminal offence (including the offence under section 3 of breaching a civil injunction when in full force: see p.146 for the authors' explanation for this). Section 5 of the 1997 Act provides:

(1) A court sentencing or otherwise dealing with a person ('the defendant') convicted of an offence under section 2 or 4 may (as well as sentencing him or dealing with him in any other way) make an order under this section.

(2) The order may, for the purpose of protecting the victim of the offence, or any other person mentioned in the order, from further conduct which—
(a) amounts to harassment, or
(b) will cause a fear of violence,
prohibit the defendant from doing anything described in the order.

A restraining order may be for a specific period or 'until further order': section 5(3).

An example of a restraining order adapted from that suggested by the Judicial Studies Board is reproduced below. (Notes accompanying the specimen form indicate that copies would be given or sent to: the defendant, the chief officer of Roddenbury police station and Jadzia Dax; and if the case involved a defendant below the age of 18 that a copy should also be sent to his or her parents and, if at school, headmaster).

RODDENBURY MAGISTRATES' COURT

RESTRAINING ORDER

On

THE DEFENDANT James Tiberius Kirk was convicted by this court of an offence contrary to s.2(1) Protection from Harassment Act 1997 and the Court made the following restraining order against the defendant under the provisions of s.5(1) Protection from Harassment Act 1997.

1) THE DEFENDANT IS PROHIBITED from making any contact either directly or indirectly with Jadzia Dax.

2) THE DEFENDANT IS PROHIBITED from entering the street known as Enterprise Crescent or from driving along it. However the defendant may walk or drive along the street twice a day on his way to work or his way back from work but he may not stop, dawdle or talk to anyone whilst travelling along Enterprise Crescent.

3) THE DEFENDANT IS PROHIBITED from contacting Jadzia Dax and from telephoning, writing, or sending E-mail to her at her home at 171 Enterprise Crescent, Smalltown or elsewhere.

THIS ORDER SHALL EXPIRE at midnight on   unless varied or discharged by this court at an earlier date.

ANY BREACH OF THIS ORDER IS AN OFFENCE contrary to s.5(5) Protection from Harassment Act 1997.

Signed etc.

Example of a restraining order

Background

Criminal courts possess longstanding powers to impose bail conditions to protect witnesses when defendants are awaiting trial or sentence. A frequent bail condition in connection with a charge of violence is one prohibiting the defendant from contacting or interfering with prosecution witnesses. However, once a defendant is convicted and sentenced, bail conditions come to an end. Section 5 represents a major development in giving criminal courts the power to impose analogous requirements *following* conviction, and comparable to those found in civil injunctions. As with non-molestation injunctions (*Chapter 3*) the terms must be precise, and capable of being readily understood and enforced.

Section 5(2)

Section 5(2) allows courts to prohibit the defendant from 'doing anything described in the order'. Nonetheless, by virtue of the same statutory provision, the purpose of the order must be *to protect the victim of the offence, or any other person mentioned in the order, from further conduct which amounts to harassment or which will cause fear of violence.*

The future behaviour which is forbidden thus need not strictly bear a direct relationship to that alleged as the basis of the offence, although it may often do so (i.e. identical behaviour will normally be forbidden). Neither, seemingly, is there any requirement that a restraining order must otherwise coincide with the conduct which is the basis of the offence, i.e. since section 5 is of general application to section 2 or 4, it might, ironically, prohibit the causing of fear of violence following a conviction under section 2; or harassment following a conviction under section 4. The order can also protect third parties 'mentioned in the order', such as children, relatives or associates—but without any statutory definition or limitations.

Where a defendant has pleaded not guilty but nonetheless has been convicted following a trial it should be clear from the evidence in the case what behaviour needs to be checked. If a defendant pleads guilty it will be important, in considering the terms of the restraining order, to know the exact facts upon which he or she did so. If the prosecutor's outline is accepted by the defendant no problem is likely to arise here; but harassment situations can be beset with conflict and if the facts are in dispute a 'Newton hearing' will need to take place to determine exactly what the true facts are: see *R v Newton* (1982) 77 Cr. App R 13. This involves a 'trial within a trial' and *ex hypothesi* the calling of evidence and this being challenged. Thus, whilst a guilty plea might be one indicator of contrition, vehement argument about the circumstances—especially if this involves the perpetrator pressing the victim in cross-examination—might equally demonstrate the case for a restraining order.

Breach of a restraining order a criminal offence

Under section 5(5) breach of a restraining order is itself an either way offence.[10] This is punishable in the Crown Court by up to five years imprisonment or an unlimited fine, or both; and on summary conviction by imprisonment of up to six months or a fine not exceeding the statutory maximum (£5,000), or both. Again, the standard powers to make other sentences and orders and an award of compensation for injury, loss or damage apply.

Acting on the breach

In the absence of procedural rules, it is advisable that courts ensure lines of communication between themselves and the police so that the latter are aware of the existence of a restraining order and its terms, and are thus able to act to bring proceedings quickly when appropriate. Naturally, the victim/survivor—who for practical reasons will need to be sent a copy of the order—can also draw this to police attention.

Variation and discharge

A restraining order can be varied or discharged on application by the prosecutor, the defendant or any other person mentioned in it: section 5(5). A beneficiary could be 'conveniently' harassed if someone subject to a restraining order made recurring applications to vary or to discharge the order. It would seem to be open to a court to treat repeat applications where no new grounds arise as an abuse of process, or as vexatious, and to refuse to hear them. Rules such as those in section 91(14) Children Act 1989—whereby a court may prohibit further applications without the leave of the court—would have put this beyond doubt but were not enacted.

Procedure

No duty is cast on the prosecutor (or anyone else) to *apply* for an order; and, strictly speaking, no power or authority to apply exists. This can be contrasted with the basic fact that the police/CPS or a private individual can bring a prosecution and with the variation provisions in section 5(4), under which the prosecutor, defendant or any other person mentioned in the order may make application (above); and the position in relation to civil injunctions under section 3 (next section).

If the court *is* considering a restraining order, natural justice indicates that the defendant should be warned of this fact—and of the

---

[10] This in itself is an unusual situation; i.e. for one sentence to precipitate another. 'Breach' could constitute a fresh offence of harassment (under section 2 or 4 of the 1997 Act); but the perpetrator could not be dealt with for both the breach and a fresh offence on the self-same facts, *semble*.

likely terms of the order—and be allowed to make representations before a final decision is arrived at.

Appeal
The normal right of appeal against sentence to the Crown Court or Court of Appeal as appropriate incorporates a challenge to a restraining order.

THE CIVIL REMEDY UNDER SECTION 3

As an alternative to pursuing criminal sanctions, harassment can be dealt with by the survivor or potential victim applying for damages and/or an injunction under section 3 of the 1997 Act for the statutory tort of harassment. This uses the same basic criteria described in relation to criminal proceedings and contained in section 1 of the 1997 Act, i.e. there must be a course of conduct amounting to harassment and actual or inferred knowledge by way of the same objective and subjective tests discussed earlier in this chapter. Civil applications may be made to the High Court or county court. Section 3 provides:

(1) An actual or apprehended breach of section 1 may be the subject of a claim in civil proceedings by the person who is or may be the victim of the course of conduct in question.
(2) On such a claim, damages may be awarded for (among other things) any anxiety caused by the harassment and any financial loss resulting from the harassment.

The civil provisions are thus wider in that the extend to an apprehended breach of section 1.[11]

Power of to apply for a warrant for the respondent's arrest
The 1997 Act gives the court further powers under section 3 as follows:

(3) Where—
(a) in such proceedings the High Court or a county court grants an injunction for the purpose of restraining the defendant from pursuing any conduct which amounts to harassment, and
(b) the plaintiff considers that the defendant has done anything which he is prohibited from doing by the injunction,

---

[11] There is always the possibility of criminal proceedings for an *attempt* to harass. With an apprehended breach under the civil provisions one incident might suffice, or even no such conduct but other evidence to ground apprehension of a breach of section 1. In effect, 'apprehension' removes the need for any actual course of conduct—but the applicant will need to establish this is what is in prospect (and that if it occured it would involve harassment).

the plaintiff may apply for the issue of a warrant for the arrest of the defendant.

This addresses a defect in the pre-existing law whereby no power of arrest could be attached to an old-style anti-harassment injunction (it still cannot, and the power to apply for a warrant is a significant improvement). The application for the defendant to be arrested can be made to the High Court if the injunction was granted by that court, or if it was granted by a county court to any county court: section 3(4).

Under section 3(3)(a) the plaintiff must consider that the defendant 'has done' something in breach of the injunction, so that a warrant of arrest cannot be issued in anticipation of a perceived future breach, or *a fortiori* at the time when the injunction itself is granted. This can be contrasted with the position in relation to the non-molestation orders etc. under Part IV of the Family Law Act 1996 when not only does the court have a jurisdiction at the time, but a power of arrest *must* normally be attached if there has been a history of violence or threats of violence (*Chapter 3*).

The application for a warrant of arrest must be substantiated on oath: section 3(5)(a); and the High Court judge or district judge may only issue the warrant if he or she 'has reasonable grounds for believing that the defendant has done anything which he is prohibited from doing by the injunction': section 3(5)(b).

Breach of a section 3 injunction

Until sub-sections 3(6) to (9) of the Act are in force, breach of an injunction will be dealt with as a contempt of court (*Chapters 2* and *6*). This is relatively disadvantageous, such procedures being cumbersome compared with the remedy provided by the as yet unimplemented provisions (as at the time of writing), or where the police can act speedily to deal with breach of a restraining order made in criminal proceedings (above). As indicated, the law is remedied to an extent by section 3(3) which enables an application to be made for a warrant of arrest—but, as yet, when arrested the defendant can only be dealt with for contempt.

Forthcoming civil remedy

All this will change once sub-sections 3(6) to 3(9) are in force. There will then be an alternative remedy for breach of the injunction due to the creation of a further new *criminal* offence. Section 3 states:

(6) Where—
(a) the High Court or a county court grants an injunction for the purpose mentioned in subsection 3(a), and

(b) without reasonable excuse the defendant does anything which he is prohibited from doing by the injunction, he is guilty of an offence.

This is an either way offence carrying a maximum penalty in the Crown Court of five years' imprisonment, an unlimited fine, or both; and on summary conviction of six months' imprisonment and/or a fine up to the statutory maximum (£5,000). The standard sentencing options for criminal offences, including compensation, apply: but see next item.

No power to make a restraining order on breach of an injunction

It should be noted that (even when in force) there is *no power to make a restraining order* on conviction of breaching a civil anti-harassment injunction. This would be largely superfluous as the civil injunction will, or can, remain in existence or can be renewed independently of the criminal enforcement proceedings. Also, any further breaches of the injunction will constitute fresh criminal offences under section 3(6).[12]

Contempt proceedings and prosecution

Section 3(7) prevents civil courts from dealing with a matter as a contempt of court where someone is convicted under the section. There is no such statutory bar where the defendant is acquitted or, say, criminal proceedings are discontinued—or, seemingly, if they relate to a different course of conduct. Conversely, neither can conviction follow if someone has been punished for contempt: section 3(8). Interestingly, there is no statutory bar to starting contempt proceedings whilst criminal proceedings are pending (or *vice versa*)—so that it is possible to envisage 'a race between courts'. Neither is there a bar to issuing a warrant of arrest for breach of an injunction pending or even following conviction under section 3(4). It would, however, seem to be an answer for the defendant to say that proceedings are pending elsewhere. One problem is that applications to civil or criminal courts are likely to be made *ex parte* (if the defendant were present in civil proceedings the power to issue a warrant in section 3(5) becomes superfluous). It seems reasonable for courts to enquire whether other proceedings are pending or contemplated and to take this into account in deciding whether to allow process. If the defendant has been charged by the police (as opposed to being proceeded against by way of information and summons) a criminal court might have to decide whether to stay those proceedings at some later stage—so that it also seems incumbent on the police to establish whether the victim has already commenced civil proceedings for breach of an injunction. It could be viewed as an abuse of process if

---

[12] They may also constitute offences under section 2 or 4, subject to a similar caveat to that in footnote 10.

the victim commences or tries to commence two sets of proceedings. Added to all this is the possibility that any fresh incident may form part of a new course of conduct upon which new proceedings, civil or criminal, might be based.

PROS AND CONS OF CRIMINAL AND CIVIL PROCEEDINGS FOR HARASSMENT

The following are among the considerations for applicants to bear in mind when deciding whether to pursue prosecution (and a restraining order) or civil proceedings (and an injunction):

- a lesser standard of proof applies to civil proceedings (on a preponderance of probabilities) as opposed to that in criminal proceedings (beyond reasonable doubt)
- a civil injunction can be granted at an interlocutory stage and is likely to be granted fairly readily
- having regard to developments in the civil law, particularly the case of *Burris v. Adzani* [1995] 4 ALL ER 802 (further discussed below), it is likely that the civil courts will adopt a liberal approach towards section 3. Criminal courts cannot do so and are far more restricted by rules of evidence and procedure.
- bail conditions can safeguard a situation in criminal proceedings pending trial or sentence
- the power of criminal courts to make the restraining order may be a factor in favour of a decision to go to the police (or bring a private prosecution)
- legal aid is not available for a private prosecution
- both orders are likely to be expressed in similar term but because the victim is always directly involved in civil proceedings an injunction may be more likely to reflect what the victim actually wants and needs. More often than not, the victim is not present in criminal proceedings, and in any case has no formal rights or influence vis-à-vis the making of a restraining order.
- section 3 covers *apprehended* as well as *actual* harassment and therefore a civil application can be made when a victim anticipates harassment in the future, rather than waiting to suffer harm before a prosecution can be brought. Again, attempts to harass or cause fear are, technically speaking, criminal offences, though seemingly an attempt to harass would often be difficult to prove in practice.
- damages may be awarded under section 3 *inter alia* for anxiety caused by harassment and any financial loss resulting from it: section 3(2). It is debatable how far compensation in a criminal

court extends in this regard; and criminal courts tend (perhaps wrongly) to be more parsimonious when it comes to compensation. Again, the victim will often not be present at the criminal court and will need to rely on the prosecutor outlining the loss, damage or injury satisfactorily and countering any excuses/challenges—or any information in a pre-sentence report (PSR): *Chapter 2.*

* the six months time limit for summary criminal offences under section 2 does not apply to civil proceedings (or to the more serious section 4 criminal proceedings). The normal time limit for personal injury proceedings is expressly abrogated by section 6 of the 1997 Act.

Burris v. Adzani

In the course of his leading judgment in *Burris v. Adzani* [1995] 4 ALL ER 802, Sir Thomas Bingham (when Master of the Rolls) repeatedly used the words 'legitimate interests' and distinguished such interests from those which can be strictly protected in tort. He made it clear that the courts will adopt a common sense approach to the subject of harassment and not necessarily seek to limit relief depending upon whether the facts fall within the principle of established tort law. It is clear that courts will restrain behaviour which would not otherwise be regarded as unlawful in order to protect the legitimate interests of an applicant/plaintiff.

In a case where the applicant's legitimate interests are being infringed by the respondent/defendant, the court has to look at whether relief by way of an injunction would affect the legitimate interests of the latter. If it would, then the court has to carry out a balance of interests test, explained by Sir Thomas Bingham (at pp.810 to 811 of the above report) as follows:

> There are two interests to be reconciled. One is that of the defendant. His liberty must be respected up to the point at which his conduct infringes or threatens to infringe the rights of the plaintiff. No restraint should be placed on him which is not judged to be necessary to protect the rights of the plaintiff, but the plaintiff has an interest which the court must be astute to protect. The rule of law requires that those whose rights are infringed should seek the aid of the court, and respect for the legal process can only suffer if those who need protection fail to get it. Respect for the freedom of the aggressor should never lead the court to deny necessary protection to the victim.

This was further explained by Lord Justice Schiemann:

> There are in these cases two interests to be reconciled — that of the plaintiff not to be harassed, that of the defendant to be allowed to move freely along

the highway. An exclusion zone interferes with the latter in order to secure the former. On its face it forbids what are lawful actions. The defendant has rendered himself liable to such an order because of his previous harassing behaviour. Nonetheless the judge imposing such an order must be careful not to interfere with the defendant's right more than is necessary in order to protect the plaintiff.

The judgement also made it clear that in adopting a balance of interests test in the end the need to protect the victim from aggression and harassment is paramount. Another important element in the ruling in *Burris v. Adzani* concerns the principles to be adopted by courts when dealing with interlocutory injunctions which are more often than not granted *ex parte* (i.e. after hearing only the person who is aggrieved). The case clarifies that courts will readily grant such relief if there is 'an arguable course of action, and (pursuant to the Supreme Court Act 1981, section 37(1)) where it appears to the court to be just and convenient'. This relatively low threshold is likely to be employed in the county court and High Court with regard to applications under section 3.

An example may assist. The actions of someone driving a motor car down a public highway are normally entirely lawful, assuming he or she has a licence to drive and complies with road traffic law and requirements. But such behaviour might be prohibited under section 3 by way of an injunction if the court felt that the behaviour infringed the legitimate interests of the applicant. This might be the case if the driver was the former spouse or partner of someone living in the particular road, and there was a background of threats or violence. Depending on the actual facts, driving up and down a road could cause a former spouse to be alarmed and distressed, such that a court would consider this to be harassment. In the spirit of *Burris v. Adzani* the court would lean towards granting an injunction, but only to the extent that this was necessary. The court would examine the legitimate interests of the defendant in driving along the road and balance these against those of the former spouse/partner. If the defendant had no cause to drive along that road for business or other legitimate purposes an injunction would seem likely. Conversely, if he lived 'three houses away' the court would need to take this competing interest into account. The degree of interference and its history would be part of this balancing exercise.

RELEVANCE OF EARLIER INCIDENTS

As already discussed the time between incidents may affect whether there is a course of conduct (see above). A further issue which falls to be considered—and which is easier to discuss now that the criminal and civil remedies have both been outlined—is that of the admissibility and relevance of previous incidents, especially where these involve criminal convictions or police cautions, warnings or reprimands.

If a defendant has been convicted and dealt with for a criminal offence which is alleged as part of a course of conduct the bare fact of conviction can be proved by way of a certificate of conviction obtainable from the criminal court. This will not prove the facts behind the conviction—the truly relevant aspect. But in what circumstances can such facts be relied upon in harassment proceedings in any event? This is an issue which is doubly complicated in a criminal case by reason of the general rule that previous convictions are not admissible to prove guilt in the present case (or, alternatively, on the ground that to receive such information in a criminal trial would be prejudicial). Also, on behalf of a defendant, it could be argued that as he or she has already been sentenced for the earlier offence, allowing it to be used to prove a later allegation would, in effect, contravene the rule against double jeopardy already mentioned in relation to section 2 prosecutions.

The contrary argument is that to prohibit evidence of behaviour from an earlier offence (whatever its status in law) would frustrate the intentions of the 1997 Act which *ex hypothesi* deals with repeat behaviour and the cumulative effects of separate incidents. A 'course of conduct' unavoidably connotes unacceptable behaviour which may or may not have involved the commission of individual criminal offences. Similarly, it can be argued that the phrase always connotes something over and above the mere facts relied on, say, to ground an earlier conviction for using threatening behaviour, something in the nature of a nexus or continuum of actions (or possibly omissions: for nowhere, in the absence of case law, is there anything to suggest that an omission cannot play a part in harassment).

If a defendant was cautioned, warned or reprimanded by the police rather than charged with an offence on an earlier occasion, the considerations differ. Although a prerequisite of such action by the police is an admission of guilt to them there is no statutory provision allowing a caution etc. to be proved by production of a certificate.[13] The corollary is that neither do any strict rules of evidence prevent details of cautions being given in support of a later criminal charge of harassment. It is an open question whether a defendant might argue that admitting

---

[13] Theoretically, the officer responsible for the record or arrest etc. could be subpeonaed to produce it in either civil or criminal proceedings — or maybe the arresting officer to give evidence, say, of attending the scene of earlier events and speaking to the defendant. Surely, the 1997 Act presupposes that this could not possibly be prejudicial in the context of establishing the course of conduct or subjective knowledge of the effect on the victim of given behaviour.

evidence of a caution in a criminal trial would be prejudicial, or that he or she accepted that caution on the understanding that matters would be at an end. However, such information could prove to be highly relevant where the case rests on the actual knowledge and subjective intentions of the defendant: see under *Harassment* and *Mental element* earlier in this chapter. However, the same comments made above concerning a course of conduct requiring something 'over and above' the mere facts of an individual incident would be equally applicable.

The problem of the admissibility of previous criminal convictions recedes in civil cases where the exclusionary rules of evidence mentioned above do not apply. Neither, it seems, would it be improper for a previous civil finding to be used as evidence in a criminal case.

STATUTORY DEFENCES AND EXEMPTIONS

Certain statutory defences are available in relation to proceedings for breach of section 1 (harassment); and to someone charged with a criminal offence under section 4 (putting people in fear of violence etc.).

Statutory defences
Where proceedings are brought under section 2 or section 3 (criminal and civil harassment, respectively) the defendant can put forward one of the statutory defences in section 1(3) which provides that:

> (3) Subsection (1) does not apply to a course of conduct if the person who pursued it shows —
> (a) that it was pursued for the purpose of preventing or detecting crime,
> (b) that it was pursued under any enactment or rule of law or to comply with any condition or requirement imposed by any person under any enactment, or
> (c) that in the particular circumstances the pursuit of the course of conduct was reasonable.

Defences under section 1(3)(a) and (b) are primarily restricted to police, officials, bailiffs, process servers and the like. That under sub-section (c) is perhaps the most likely defence to be raised in a domestic context.[14]

---

[14] Raising issues of reasonable seems to require the court to consider little more than it will be doing in any event if applying an objective test (pp.134, 136) or if applying the 'balance of interests' approach in *Burris v Adzani* or looking at 'legitimate interests' (p.148). When applying a subjective test, a defence of reasonableness might, if *bona fide*, be the answer to the unduly sensitive victim ('I knew my genuine attempts to discuss matters were having that effect, but she seemed to over-react — and I still felt that I had to reason with her') (p.134).

It is worth noting that there is no defence of engaging in a lawful occupation, such as a journalism. Such people would have to rely on their actions being reasonable in the particular circumstances under section 1(3)(c).

The section 1 defences which legitimise a course of conduct are restricted to harassment within the meaning of sections 1 and 7—and are not apposite to the more serious offence under section 4 (putting people in fear etc.).

Defences to the criminal offence under section 4

Section 4 contains a number of comparable defences which are exclusively referable to the criminal offence created by that provision. Section 4(3) provides:

(3) It is a defence for a person charged with an offence under this section to show that—

(a) his course of conduct was pursued for the purpose of preventing or detecting crime,

(b) his course of conduct was pursued under any enactment or rule of law or to comply with any condition or requirement imposed by any person under any enactment, or

(c) the pursuit of his course of conduct was reasonable for the protection of himself or another or for the protection of his or another's property.

The significant variation is that between section 1(3)(c) and section 4(3)(c), the latter defining what is acceptable, the former leaving matters to the court's discretion when assessing reasonableness.

Exemption from liability

Under section 12 of the 1997 Act, the secretary of state may certify that in his or her opinion '. . . anything done by a specified person on a specified occasion' related to national security, or the economic well being of the United Kingdom, or the prevention or detection of serious crime, and that it was done on behalf of the Crown'.[15] Such a certificate is conclusive evidence that the 1997 Act does not apply to any conduct of the person concerned 'on that occasion'. Proceedings in such cases are unlikely to come before the court at all unless brought by individuals privately. If they do, the practical effect of section 12 is to nullify them. The document purporting to be a certificate must be received in evidence unless it is proved that it is not such: section 12(3).

---

[15] *Quare* whether James Bond could escape harassment of his current partner carried out within the context of events primarily directed towards state security.

COMPARISON WITH PART IV FLA 1996

When the Family Law Act 1996 and the Protection From Harassment Act 1997 are both fully in force there will be a true overlap in the remedies available to victims of domestic violence, harassment and molestation. 'Harassment' under the 1997 Act appears to be similar to the concept of 'molestation' in the 1996 Act (or at least the former encompasses the latter) and therefore a survivor or potential victim could on some occasions consider:

- an application for a non-molestation order under Part IV of the 1996 Act; or

- an application under section 3 Protection from Harassment Act 1997; or

- a prosecution for an offence under section 2 (or may be even section 4) of the 1997 Act.

The main differences between the remedies provided by the two Acts are as follows:

- only 'associated persons' can apply under Part IV of the Family Law Act 1996 for a non-molestation order. If a stranger is harassing a victim the remedy will lie under the 1997 Act.

- if people *are* 'associated' the criteria under the two Acts are different. The open criteria discussed in *Burris v. Adzani* (p.148) are likely to be applied by analogy to applications under section 3, whereas the criteria in the Family Law Act 1996 require the court to have regard to 'all the circumstances including the need to secure the health, safety and well being of the applicant or the person for whose benefit the order will be made and of any relevant child'. It is noticeable therefore that specific mention of the relevant child is not found under the 1997 Act, although the balance of legitimate interests of the plaintiff and defendant are likely to involve consideration of the needs of any children in respect of any application under section 3. Further—as indicated above—an order under the 1997 Act can also be used to protect third parties, including children. Events which affect third parties, including children, can be taken into account and dealt with under either law.

- any injunction granted by the court under section 3 of the 1997 Act cannot initially contain a power of arrest. Only if the injunction is breached, can the plaintiff apply for a warrant of arrest; whereas in respect of a non-molestation order a power of arrest *must* normally be granted if there has been violence or a threat of violence

- a court dealing with family proceedings can make a non-molestation order of its own motion. There is no power to make injunctions of the court's own motion under section 3 of the 1997 Act, only on application (this contrasting also with the position on conviction under section 2 or 4 in relation to a restraining order).

Useful provisions

The indications are that the provisions of the 1997 Act are being well used in both civil and criminal courts (if somewhat patchily, in the latter case, by police forces). What this chapter discloses is that the provisions, if properly understood and applied—and with evidence presented in a way which matches the requirements outlined—provide an effective remedy with which to confront a wide range of personal interference.

CHAPTER 8

Strategies for Preventing Domestic Violence

In broad terms the policies and measures outlined in earlier chapters of this book have the twin aim of:

- responding to domestic violence when it occurs (or whenever possible before it occurs) via a range of legal powers—some recent or enhanced;

- seeking, by various means, to ensure that domestic violence (or further violence) does not happen.

In this latter preventive context, various powers exist to pre-empt attacks, threats or similarly intrusive behaviour or to stop it escalating into something worse. Even under the criminal jurisdiction, the restraining order available following conviction for harassment (*Chapter 7*) is clearly intended to be preventive in nature.

GOVERNMENT POLICY

All this accords with government strategies, the joint Cabinet Office/Home Office publication *Living Without Fear*[1] placing future action in relation to domestic violence firmly within the arena of community safety, women's safety and the prevention of crime. First and foremost, that initiative is part of the government's Crime Reduction Programme. Secondly, the government has expressed its determination to achieve long-term improvements, principally through survivor networks relying upon—as variously described—'integrated', 'multi-agency', 'partnership' or 'cross-cutting' strategies. Joint-working by the relevant statutory and non-statutory agencies is thus the lynch-pin of future attempts to reduce domestic violence. It is also important to emphasise certain other key points which go beyond the bare legalities:

- the government has set a timescale of five years 'within which there will be effective multi-agency partnerships operating right across the country'

---

[1] *Living Without Fear: An Integrated Approach to Tackling Violence Against Women*, 1999: see *Chapter 1*

- these partnerships will draw on good practice (some examples are noted later in this chapter) to prevent risk to women's personal safety. Above all, practitioners need to be alert to the needs of women who seek help, something which the government intends to achieve via:

  — publicity initiatives, including the nationwide *Break the Chain* campaign mentioned in *Chapter 1*. To an extent this aspect is also linked by government with the notion of 'zero tolerance' and the wider purpose of changing attitudes towards violence against women.[2] Similarly, education and awareness raising in schools (including the encouragement of resource packs) again seek to develop appropriate attitudes by boys and men towards women:

    Personal, Social and Health Education (PSHE) provides the opportunity to give young people behavioural and relationship education in schools. This can benefit many aspects of their lives, including confirmation of the unacceptability of violence within relationships.

  — routine questioning by a range of front-line staff involving questions being asked in appropriate circumstances by all relevant professionals to encourage earlier identification of domestic violence as an underlying cause of problems. This general increase in awareness is also intended to extend to organizations such as the Benefits Agency which recognises '. . . the importance of providing a supportive service to those of our customers who, at any time, have been the victims of domestic violence'.[3]

  — good practice initiatives to publicise help and support. Local information leaflets now exist in many areas. The government instances information being provided via such straightforward and everyday outlets as maternity packs, community safety key-rings and the reverse of car park tickets. Also, the Women's Aid Federation (*Chapter 3*) has launched a *Gold Book*, a UK-wide directory of domestic violence and helpline services (whilst Broadcast Support Services produces a

---

[2] The items listed in our bullet points from here onwards are taken from *Chapter 4* of *Living Without Fear*, which deals with each of these at some length. The summaries are our own and do not necessarily use the exact or full terminology of the government's proposals.

[3] A significant proportion of survivors claim benefits, often through losing pre-existing resources. One reason why people stay in an abusive relationship is because they wonder how they might manage financially: *Break the Chain*, p.5.

Survivors Directory listing counselling services for victims of sexual abuse in Britain and Ireland).

- the development of projects (within the Crime Reduction Programme) to address domestic violence, rape and sexual assault. Under each heading, funding streams for projects and other initiatives are to be announced and bids sought (the fact of a £6 million pound investment was mentioned in *Chapter 1*). This will involve 'a more transparent system' for funding women's refuges and other key support services. The government proposes:

> . . . to introduce an integrated policy and funding framework for support services, *Supporting People*. This will bring together local housing, social and probation services to work in partnership to plan and fund support services for survivors of domestic violence and other vulnerable groups. . .

- monitoring and support measures directed towards practitioners and including:

— fresh guidance promoting pro-active inter-agency partnerships

— a new database of women's refuges and services around the country by the end of 1999 together with the more stable funding mechanism already indicated above (We outlined the problems faced by women who are fleeing from violence in *Chapter 3*)

— a more consistent approach to the collection and use of data

— performance indicators for statutory services including the police and new guidance, including on the effectiveness of pro-arrest policies and tackling attrition (*Chapter 2*). The government instances as an example of good practice the Killingbeck project, an early intervention model developed by West Yorkshire Police which operates a three stage response—directed at perpetrators and victims—and which has reduced repeat victimisation.[4]

---

[4] *Level 1:* police attendance, letters to victim and perpetrator, and an information card of local contacts; *Level 2* (second attendance): letters, an officer visits the woman and, with consent, instigates 'Cocoon Watch' (a variation on Neighbourhood Watch). *Level 3* (third attendance or above): letters, a visit by the Domestic Violence Officer and Police Watch (regular drive-by on patrol). Other interventions may be linked to any of these and where the offence is serious (the scheme distinguishes 'common law' and 'criminal' offences) arrest will normally occur immediately. Research on the project has been conducted by the Research Centre on Violence, Abuse and Gender Relations at Leeds Metropolitan University: see *Arresting Evidence: Domestic Violence and Repeat Victimisation*, Jalna Halmer, Sue Griffiths and David Jerwood, Police Research Series, Paper 104, London, Home Office, 1999.

- training in sensitivity for a whole range of practitioners including police, Crown prosecutors, the judiciary and lawyers. This is scheduled to include overhauled guidance in most areas of violence against women and specialist training for prosecutors dealing with sexual offences. More generally the government urges improved guidance and training for *all* people working in the domestic violence arena and, in particular, that all agencies should:

  — train new and existing staff to provide an appropriate and sensitive service;

  — ensure that staff training is periodically refreshed and updated;

  — identify women who may be seeking services as a result of domestic violence;

  — ensure that all women are aware of the support and help available;

  — encourage women to come forward;

  — ensure that the service is accessible to all women who need it, and that barriers such as language and disability are overcome;

  — ensure women's safety;

  — maintain confidentiality;

  — establish appropriate recording systems; and

  — evaluate and review performance including complaints.[5]

- providing information, advice and advocacy including encouragement of the 'one stop shop' so that women do not have to contact several different agencies before receiving help. The government instances as an example of good practice the Croydon Domestic Violence Survivors Panel and One Stop Shop where a panel of survivors advises the local inter-agency domestic violence forum: 'The panel has played a key role in initiating and developing Croydon's One Stop Shop Service that provides an integrated service to survivors of domestic violence. Members of the panel operate a "friends" system to provide support to women coming forward to the One Stop Shop for Help'.

  Other examples of good practice instanced by government are Domestic Violence Matters in Islington which was designed to provide civilian support workers alongside police and the

---

[5] *Living Without Fear*, p.57

Nottingham Women's Centre which provides a range of women's community initiatives and self-help projects as well as a specialist helpline, outreach and advice services and 'a safe and "non-stigmatising"[6] point of access'.

Also included within a forward-looking communications strategy is the work of Victim Support, with over 400 local schemes throughout the UK providing information, practical help and emotional support to people affected by crime. As indicated in *Chapter 1*, the government is increasing the grant to that organization to £19 million—part of which will enable the extension of support services for victims and witnesses (similar to those which already exist in the Crown Court) to magistrates' courts nationwide.

- violence helplines as mentioned in *Chapter 1*: the aim is for these to be available nationwide and, assuming a proper level of viability, to operate 24 hours per day.[7] The government is committed to improving accessibility including looking at the resource implications of extending to a round-the-clock service those helplines currently operating at a lesser level.

- community alarms which women known to be at risk of further attack can be given and which bring 'an automated pre-arranged response as part of an overall safety plan' (although the government notes that these are not infallible and that their use is often time-limited or radius-limited).[8]

- a raft of other initiatives, including: theatre workshops, special arrangements for rural areas, encouraging good practice in relation to media and television images, creating safer communities generally, and awareness-raising for personal safety

- what is described as a 'kick start' to the process by way of a national conference for senior criminal justice system professionals

---

[6] i.e. seemingly meaning 'non-publicised' (authors' comment)

[7] The current national helplines are: the Women's Aid Domestic Violence Helpline (0345 023 468); Refuge's 24-Hour National Crisis Line (0990 995 443); and Victim Supportline (0845 30 30 900).

[8] These includes 'panic alarms' (a pendant or silent unit connected to an existing telephone line and which can be connected to the police or other alarm service); 'Tunstall alarms' (which activate a recording device which may produce potential evidence); and 'mobile 999 phones'. The government also instances as one example of good practice a range of linklines, partnerships which seek to join established services to alarm systems.

in November 1999 to address all forms of violence against women, followed by regional seminars to share and promulgate practical and innovative ways of working.

Domestic violence fora

In terms of integrated approaches, the report also identifies a wide range of individual initiatives, as to which the government makes the following points:

> There are already around 200 inter-agency domestic violence fora[9] across England and Wales. Each agency provides an appropriate response to women who have experienced violence and effective referral networks are used . . . We see the sort of inter-agency partnership represented by domestic violence fora as the way forward. Later this year we will be issuing inter-departmental guidance to agencies dealing with domestic violence. The guidance will emphasise the importance of agencies working in partnership. It will include practical advice on how such partnerships might be established and operate, the role of domestic violence fora, the issues that are likely to arise, and how common problems might be avoided . . .

The central role of integrated services is again emphasised in the concluding words of *Living With Fear* when the government pledges its commitment to a clear framework for action:

> Within five years we expect to see effective violence against women partnerships operating across the country. We stand ready to support a new range of projects under the Crime Reduction Programme which will further lead the way. But above all, we move into a new era where we no longer sweep violence against women under the carpet; where women can seek and find the help they need without fear of shame or retribution; and where we all, public and voluntary sector, the justice system and national and local agencies of all kinds pull together to build a better society.

GOOD PRACTICE AND PERPETRATORS

What then should happen in relation to perpetrators of domestic violence (an appropriate level of sentence for criminal offences apart)? According to the government:

> In order to reduce violence, the behaviour and attitudes of perpetrators must change. There is much debate about the effectiveness of perpetrator

---

[9] Hackney Domestic Violence Forum, e.g. has produced *Domestic Violence: A Guide for Service Providers* which details local services. There are similar initiatives in many parts of the country.

programmes, with different studies producing inconsistent results. We need to build on best practice to promote those that are effective.

Living Without Fear instances several examples of good practice ranging from the North Hampshire Perpetrators Project, a 30 week group work programme which receives referrals from probation officers, the courts, statutory agencies and voluntary organizations (also self-referrals) and offers parallel services for survivors to National Practitioners' Network principles—designed to guide services running perpetrator projects and which place the safety of women and children uppermost.

Standing Together Against Domestic Violence

One particular good practice intervention model instanced by government is the Hammersmith and Fulham Domestic Violence Forum pilot project Standing Together Against Domestic Violence which is based on the 'Domestic Abuse Intervention Project' (DAIP) in Duluth, USA (the Duluth approach). We are indebted to members of the Inner London Probation Service (ILPS)[10] for additional information about this project which operates in partnership with other domestic violence programmes initiated by ILPS (see the note on the Camberwell Violence Prevention Project, below) and seeks to develop a co-ordinated response to domestic violence in Fulham and Hammersmith.

The project operates as a partnership of criminal justice, public sector and community agencies within the borough of Hammersmith and Fulham and involves the council's Community Safety Unit.[11] It is steered by a multi-agency Domestic Violence Forum and, in turn, through the forum's Criminal Justice sub-group. It is instructive, now that we have dealt with many aspects of domestic violence in earlier chapters, to revisit what domestic violence consists of by noting the council's own definition:[12]

Domestic violence involves the physical, sexual emotional and mental abuse of women by men with whom they are or have been in a relationship. This violence may be actual, threatened or attempted . . . An individual woman's experience of domestic violence is unique and may involve a combination of physical, sexual, emotional and mental abuse. What is common to all women's experience of domestic violence is that the abusers may use

---

[10] The authors would like to thank Peter Jeffries and Fiona Morton.

[11] In terms of action by local authorities and other social landlords it is interesting to note Eliabeth Burney's findings concerning a trend towards seeking to curtail anti-social behaviour—including domestic violence—by contract, breach of the terms of which may lead to eviction: see *Crime and Banishment: Nuisance and Exclusion in Social Housing*, Waterside Press, 1999.

[12] As contained in the council's published 'Policy on Domestic Violence'.

humiliation, threats and/or force to control the women and children in their household.

The essential multi-agency nature of the initiative can be seen from the fact that it is a partnership between the local authority, police, CPS, local courts, ILPS (a major contributor to funding), Women's Aid, the local Law Centre, Fulham Parents and Children, Domestic Violence Intervention Programme (DVIP) and Awareness in Practice. It was the first project of its kind in the United Kingdom to seek to put all the elements of a Duluth approach in place at once, and thus will provide a valuable testing ground for other communities and criminal justice agencies wishing to develop a co-ordinated community response.

The project aims to put in place a number of practical, policy, procedural and service measures in order, among other things, to:

- improve safety for those subject to domestic violence, from the moment of first contact with the criminal justice system—e.g. via a 999 call—through to the period after the abuser completes his sentence

- increase an offenders' accountability for his actions

- deliver more effective prosecution and sentencing of abusers; and

- strengthen the public message that domestic violence is a crime which will not be tolerated.

Sentenced perpetrators attend a Violence Prevention Project (see p.164) as a requirement ('condition') of a probation order or of release from prison on licence.[13]

'Advocates', evidence gathering and emergency facilities
In practice, the scheme operates through what are known as 'advocates'.[14] The role of the advocate is to support victims during the critical first 24 hours after a woman has called the police and then throughout the court process. This is intended, among other things, to reduce the attrition rate (*Chapter 2*) so that a greater number of perpetrators come before the criminal courts. In tandem with this, the police have changed the way they respond to domestic violence and now focus on gathering corroborative evidence that will support the victim's

---

13 As with many such local initiatives there is also an element of self-referral or referral by probation officers even though no conditions have been imposed (when the completion/success tends to be lower: see later in the chapter).
14 Compare the 'friends' initiative in Croydon: see p.158.

assertions during prosecution. This is intended to reduce the extent to which the focus and the resulting pressures are upon the live evidence of the victim/survivor: the enhanced evidence gathering scheme requires officers, as appropriate, to take appropriate samples for forensic analysis; to interview neighbours and other potential witnesses; to make video recordings/take photographs of the scene; to record the alleged perpetrator's response to the woman's claims; and to work with advocates to maximise the woman's safety. The local women's refuge offers emergency overnight accommodation where necessary.

The Crown prosecutor then works closely with the police to ensure that the case is prepared effectively for court, and a set of protocols has been developed to ensure that information is exchanged appropriately between *all* agencies—so that the victim is properly protected during this crucial time and also holds the alleged perpetrator accountable. A senior Crown prosecutor oversees all domestic violence cases. The local court, whilst maintaining its judicial independence, is keen to ensure that survivors are given adequate facilities at court and keeps itself informed about the work of the pilot and the local domestic violence forum.

Applications for charitable funding have been successful—and the resulting grants will allow the employment of additional advocates, a co-ordinator and a 'tracker'. The last mentioned individual's role is to track each case through the criminal justice system and draw together monitoring statistics for the pilot project as well as ensuring that there are no 'institutional blocks'. A computer programme is being developed via a separate grant from the DAPHNE initiative (European funding).

Domestic violence courses
As part of its overall Probation Service responsibilities (but extending beyond the strict limits of these), ILPS offers a 26-week group work programme to men who have been convicted of offences involving domestic violence—and a parallel service is then offered to current partners or ex-partners of men on the programme.[15] A number of voluntary agencies offer advice and support in addition.

Rationale for the Duluth approach
The Standing Together Project is predicated among other things on a number of key points:

- on the basis of women survivor's accounts, all criminal justice interventions (fine, probation, imprisonment) appear to have some

---

[15] The programme accepts a restricted number of voluntary/self-referral cases. Experience suggests that their attendance/completion/success rate is lower than that for men attending under the compulsion of a court order.

positive effect on the behaviour of perpetrators during a 12 month follow up

- however, according to their partners, only 33 per cent of men participating in a perpetrators programme committed another violent act against their partner during the 12 month follow up period. In comparison 75 per cent of men subject to other types of sanction committed a violent act in the same period.

- Perpetrators programmes were also more successful than other forms of court disposal in reducing the *frequency* of violence—only seven per cent of men participating in the programmes, compared with 37 per cent of men sanctioned in other ways, initiated five or more violent incidents during the follow up period

- in contrast to the partners of men experiencing other sanctions, partners of those who participated in perpetrators programmes reported a significant reduction in the coercive and controlling behaviour often associated with violence against women

- court mandated programmes are more effective as offenders complete the programme. Eighty-one per cent of court mandated men attended ten to 13 sessions of DVIP's Violence Prevention Progamme compared to 43 per cent of self referral men.[16]

Violence Prevention Project

ILPS also oprates a Violence Prevention Project at its Camberwell Probation Centre, which for perpetrators again means that they attend under the compulsion of conditions attached either to a probation order or to a licence under the statutory scheme for early release from prison. According to ILPS' own research, of 93 assigned to the Camberwell programme between October 1997 and June 1999 (and with a current caseload of 68), 25 men had completed 22 sessions, only two had been re-arrested for domestic violence, only one re-convicted of domestic violence, there had been two breaches for non-attendance with nine breaches pending, and one person had been referred for individual counselling. Some voluntary probation clients attended the centre when the number of non-attenders was three (i.e. higher, in proportion).

---

[16] For the propositions and findings noted in this summary see *Re-education Programmes for Violent Men: An Evaluation*, Dobash R *et al*, Research Findings No 46, Home Office; *Supporting Women and Challenging Men: An Evaluation of the Domestic Violence Project*, Burton *et al*, Rowntree Trust, 1997.

INFORMAL MECHANISMS CONTRASTED

Preventing crime—or perhaps more to the point and in line with modern trends dealing with 'anti-social behaviour'—is, as can be detected in many government strategies, something which now features prominently in relation to a wide range of conduct and the message is that these strategies must be 'pro-active' or 'positive'. There is thus a quantum leap between solid legal remedies and compulsory programmes of the kind operated via domestic violence forums (and also in certain prisons) and less formal or non-compulsory mechanisms. But domestic violence is often intertwined with forms of conflict which are otherwise amenable to informal resolution and the strands of violence may not surface until one of those 'domestic violence aware' practitioners (see earlier in this chapter) recognises the signs. It would thus be wrong to omit information about developments which are taking place.

Inherent difficulties
Perhaps the single biggest problem in relation to human behaviour altogether is that of accurately predicting what direction it will take—in the present context who is likely to resort to violence or, where someone has already done so, whether they will return to violence in future. This is so for even stronger reasons in relation to *domestic* violence due to the very nature of day-to-day family/household existence where the parties are usually in close proximity to one another, the many forms that the violence may take, the fact that other people may see only the presentable side of a volatile relationship, and the many possible, often minute but highly sensitive triggers which it is difficult for an outsider to recognise, let alone identify with or comprehend. The business of 'risk prediction' is notoriously fallible and contentious, whilst a great degree of effort and expense can be expended on people who do not need it.[17] Nonetheless, some informal approaches have been criticised for placing victims at unacceptable risk—in danger—and even of assisting

---

[17] For an extreme scenario see *Murderers and Life Imprisonment*, Eric Cullen and Tim Newell, Waterside Press, 1999, particularly *Chapter 6*, 'Lifer Risk Assessment' by Roland Woodward. Although, in broad terms, murderers are far more likely to kill someone they know (often a partner or former partner) than a stranger, they represent an unusually low risk in terms of 'repeating' their offence or offending in other ways. Nonetheless—as noted in *Chapter 1* of this work—it is the ever present fear that violence may escalate and the fact that any violence can have non-controllable effects which causes a high degree of reservation about informal schemes.

perpetrators to weigh up the best way, to intimidate a survivor or to continue with violence in a more calculated and less visible fashion.

Mediation and conflict resolution

Although mediation services and schemes offering alternative dispute resolution (ADR) have proliferated in relation to many types of conflict in recent years, they tend to be the exception in relation to violence.[18]

A broad remit under the Family Law Act 1996

There is no general statutory scheme for mediation, counselling etc., although such activities may be carried out by statutory bodies as part of their wider remit and public duties, as well as by the voluntary sector. The one exception is that contained in Part III of the Family Law Act 1996, which seeks to divert expenditure away from costly—often bitter and protracted—litigation towards helping parties to reach a negotiated, agreed and hopefully firmer and more acceptable outcome on divorce and in relation to matters under the Children Act 1989 (particularly who a child is to reside with and future contact with a parent[19]). Initially, official commitment to the use of mediation was clear from the Green Paper *Looking to the Future: Mediation and the Grounds for Divorce* (1993):

> The system of resolving disputes through partisan arms length negotiations draws families into conflict at a time of considerable stress in their lives. Family mediation offers an alternative which has the effect of reducing tension while encouraging a couple to reach agreement on the way they must inevitably reorganize their lives and those of their children. Out of court mediation has been shown to have some particularly positive effects.

Since the Family Law Act 1996, there have been a number of pilot projects to test the viability of mediation facilities in disputes relating to family matters, including divorce,[20] non-molestation and occupation of the family home (*Chapter 3*);[21] and with regard to the Children Act 1989.

As indicated in *Chapter 1*, domestic violence is present in a high percentage of divorce cases and other family disputes, so that to this extent issues around violent behaviour unavoidably fall within this remit. Furthermore, the Family Law Act 1996 allows the Legal Aid Board to 'secure mediation' *before considering the grant of legal aid* for court

---

[18] Some adherents of restorative justice argue for more constructive and inclusionary approaches to crime, including violence when appropriate: see, generally, *Restoring Respect For Justice*, Martin Wright, Waterside Press, 1999

[19] See footnote 27 and *Appendix II*

[20] As to the law pre and post the 1996 Act

[21] As to the law post the 1996 Act

proceedings.[22] In some cases therefore, the parties to a divorce case will not get legal aid unless mediation has first been attempted and it is thus difficult to see how, in some cases, violent aspects from a marriage can be avoided by the mediator—albeit it may be a reason for reporting that mediation has been unsuccessful, is not appropriate or possible, or even that there is danger in continuing (which should, perhaps, be a point uppermost in the mind of the mediator).

The Legal Aid Board can also *offer*, but cannot insist upon, this alternative approach in cases under Part IV of the 1996 Act (non-molestation and occupation of the family home: *Chapter 3*) or under Parts IV and V of the Children Act 1989 (e.g. applications for care or supervision orders, or emergency protection orders: *Chapter 2*).

It is likely that Part III mediation will be franchised to various bodies (including firms of solicitors or barristers' chambers, as well as to existing mediation bodies) and a code of practice will apply to such mediators.

At the time of writing it has been indicated by the Lord Chancellor that pilot mediation projects have proved to be less welcome by would be divorcees than was anticipated and it is at present uncertain whether or to what extent this aspect of conflict resolution will be pursued.

Terminology

It is important to be precise about what it is that is being talked about. In connection with the Family Support Service introduced by the 1996 Act, three aspects need to be distinguished:

- *information meetings:* which will take place prior to divorce
- *counselling:* assistance towards reconciliation; and
- *mediation:* assistance in negotiating outcomes to family disputes rather than resorting to litigation.

Practitioners need to be precise in their use of terminology, and to be familiar with services in their own area. Both information meetings and counselling are likely to continue whatever the future direction of divorce mediation.

---

[22] Legal aid is also means tested. People paying for their own lawyer, or not wishing to be represented by one, will, if they choose, be able to move directly to court proceedings (equally, of course, such people will not receive financial assistance if mediation facilities *are* desired. However, the Lord Chancellor can make grants in connection with the general provision of 'marriage support services').

Not all embracing

The statutory mediation schemes only encompass certain litigants, and in some cases only on a voluntary (or 'offer') basis. Single sex partners fall completely outside the statutory scheme except where the parties are 'associated' people who are in dispute due to alleged molestation or occupation of the family home: *Chapter 3*. Other non-criminal arguments between single sex couples will need to be settled via the ordinary civil courts (where, non-statutory mediation schemes may well exist due to a general proliferation of ADR strategies). There is nothing to propel such parties in the direction of the civil courts at all: the FLA 1996 apart only where there is a contractual arrangement (still relatively unusual) requiring some judicial decision, or where children are involved (not that uncommon in a same sex relationship), is there any reason why domestic violence might be identified. Violent strands which might have been picked up on through compulsory statutory mediation may thus be missed altogether.

Family conflict in general

In *Conflict Resolution: A Foundation Guide*,[23] Susan Stewart identifies the broad range of schemes which now cater for ADR procedures including those which operate between neighbours, in schools, across faiths, cultures, in relation to the environment, employment and internationally. She points out that as many as three-quarters of family mediation services function in partnership with the probation service.[24] According to Susan Stewart, in relation to domestic violence:

> Mediators in family conflicts have to be sensitive to the possibility that domestic violence may be part of the problem. While most mediation services do not feel that disputes in which domestic violence is present can be mediated, a response from a mediation service in the south-west gave domestic violence as one of its fields of activity. This voluntary service has worked closely with local police to develop the option of mediation in domestic violence cases. The coordinator in question stressed that only professionally qualified staff work with domestic violence cases, which require skills beyond those held by most volunteer community mediators.

There is a Family Mediators' Association (FMA) whose members, lawyer mediators and family mediators in private practice, specialise in working with couples involved in separation and divorce. The FMA offers a dual

---

[23] Susan Stewart, *Conflict Resolution: A Foundation Guide,* Waterside Press, 1998. See, in particular, *Chapter 4* of that work.

[24] Which has a statutory responsibility to provide a Family Court Welfare Service. See, generally, Dick Whitfield, *Introduction to the Probation Service,* Waterside Press, 1998.

model of mediation in which two mediators work together, one a solicitor mediator and the other a family mediator usually from a social work or counselling background. FMA mediators, whether lawyers or not, are qualified to undertake All Issues Mediation. The Solicitors' Family Law Association (SFLA), an association of some 3,500 solicitors working in family cases, view mediation as an integral part of its members procedures for separating and divorcing couples. The need to have in place a credible supervisory and regulatory system for mediation is an issue which has been addressed among others by the UK College of Family Mediators. The SFLA also recognises that 'solicitors who wish to mediate need to undergo appropriate training and to be subject to a regime involving consultancy (rather than supervision as such), accreditation and regulation'.

COUNSELLING

Many of the schemes so far described may involve elements of counselling for perpetrators or victims within some broader overall objective. As emphasised throughout this work, the incidence of and potential for domestic violence presents a dilemma in terms of any attempts to deal with such violence, whether or not linked to criminal, civil or family-law based legal powers. A common problem where violence *has* been used is that of denial or justification, considerations which do not sit well with preventive work with potentially dangerous people. How can anyone trust the question (really an assertion of innocence): 'What's the problem?'

Prevention, of any kind, is virtually impossible if the perpetrator is not prepared or able to come to terms with the behaviour in question. This is a natural pre-condition before further discussion can begin concerning e.g. what triggers violent impulses, how to deal with them and alternative ways of channelling energy and aggression. It is also the case that the very notion of counselling can, if poorly handled, convey all the wrong signals: about the seriousness the behaviour in question; the true level of opprobrium which acts of violence should rightly attract (which government strategy would now seem to acknowledge). Other regular pitfalls which anyone attempting to deal with violent behaviour in this way must allow for include:

- the risk of failing to prioritise the safety of a partner or children, particularly if the perpetrator continues to live in the same domestic environment, or if he has ready access to the family members concerned

- the fact that a perpetrator may play on the seeming naiveté of those who are trying to help, by using information gleaned in counselling sessions, discussion, therapy or group work to increase the opportunity and potential for violence—to take advantage and to better cover his tracks so as to enhance a regime of terror or intimidation

- the fact that victims may be made to feel more vulnerable than before during the inevitable period of uncertainty about how the perpetrator will respond to attempts at a solution.

Questions also arise about where priorities lie, the protection of the victim or the rehabilitation/attitudinal and behavioural changes of the perpetrator: which leads on to further difficult questions concerning confidentiality, professional privilege, monitoring and evaluation of outcomes. There is also the problem that a practitioner, counsellor, mediator etc, may (notwithstanding professional training) drift into becoming a party to the conflict, a focus for recriminations and blame, the conduit for the victim's complaints, with the added risk that the involvement of an outsider—particularly 'the authorities'—may cause additional resentment between perpetrator and victim. What is openly discussed in counselling might then be revisited with a vengeance having become the basic fuel of new reasons for domestic conflict, or serve to aggravate existing tensions.

The Everyman Centre, Plymouth

It is considerations of this type which have caused some people to say that certain less formal approaches should be avoided altogether. However, according to Calvin Bell of the Everyman Centre in Plymouth, a practitioner in cognitive analytic therapy and an experienced trainer in domestic violence against women and working with men who harm:

> . . . the assessment and management of risk and the prioritisation of safety of female partners of prospective male clients referred because of relationship difficulties or violence should be fully adopted, despite its particular, legal, professional and ethical dilemmas, if we are to avoid counselling which is naive, collusive and potentially dangerous.

Given this high level of caution, the Everyman Centre was among the first (of relatively few ventures, even now) in the UK to focus on confronting domestic violence as opposed to simply identifying its existence and setting up broad mechanisms in an attempt to limit its incidence, such as providing psycho-social counselling for men who are violent and support services for their partners.[25] As Calvin Bell acknowledges, '. . . there is as yet little research-based knowledge as to what works; we are operating on the frontier of our understanding'. The centre recognises problems of the type already mentioned because:

> . . . however well-intentioned, the mere offer of counselling for the abusive man may well result in exposure of his partner to risk that would otherwise have been avoided by her leaving or staying away. Moreover, the proclivity of many men who batter to discharge their stress by being abusive to vulnerable members of their family, should not be overlooked. Where such a man having a history of severe violence to his partner is coerced or even persuaded to participate in counselling (very few attend without strong *external* motivators) that he may well experience as challenging and therefore stressful, his potential for harm-doing must be considered high, especially as many men who batter hold *their partners* directly responsible for finding themselves "in treatment". Ironically too, the man's participation in out-patient or non-custodial counselling intended to abate victimisation can also result in a reduction of perceived seriousness with which he is viewed by other statutory and voluntary agencies . . . often precipitating a minimisation or withdrawal of victim support services.

It is an understanding of such dynamics that has enabled the Everyman Centre to press ahead with intensive schemes despite a further recognition that there is a paucity of reference points and research concerning risk assessment. There are other reasons such as the perhaps not so obvious fact that some perpetrators, including those with 'homicidal urges' actually find comfort in the fact that 'some external controls will be imposed to minimise the risk of their feelings being acted upon'. The centre also recognises that the victim—often, through proximity to and knowledge of the perpetrator, the person best placed to predict risk—may have difficulties which equally require attention: few abused women indicate violence as a major problem in a relationship *unless directly questioned about its presence* (viz: the government's current strategy of making all practitioners 'domestic violence aware', above). Neither, historically speaking, have survivors been provided with adequate information about what is happening re the perpetrator: and there is an effect on the victim of accepting the perpetrator into counselling in the first place. The Everyman Centre has also recognised

---

[25] The information in this section stems from a direct personal communication from Calvin Bell. Strangely, despite its renown, the Everyman Centre does not figure in *Living Without Fear*—possibly because it could be seen as non-coercive, too reconciliatory or maybe too high risk? For further information, the address is Everyman Centre, 6 Victoria Place, Millbay Road, Plymouth, PL1 3LP. Tel: 01752 222922; E-mail: everyman.centre@virgin.net

the importance of warnings and intervention, notwithstanding the general rule that a counsellor's fundamental professional responsibility is 'to foster a client's autonomy and therefore not to interfere in his or her affairs'.

Dealing with such 'practice tensions', Calvin Bell comments that these exist because firstly:

> at a practical level, for counselling to be effective it requires an environment in which clients feel able to take the risk of exploring issues which they may never have previously discussed. Though client/counsellor confidentiality has never been absolute . . . and of the possibility of counsellors being required by the courts to disclose privileged information . . . the working precept of most generic counsellors is that the efficacy of the therapeutic alliance increases in proportion to the extent of confidentiality: honesty should be rewarded with privacy.

Secondly there is the question of 'the ethical frame' and the extent to which breaking any confidences can prejudice a client's civil liberties. However:

> Not all abusive clients have contact with their partners during counselling, some may not be in a relationship at the time and not all have a high potential for dangerousness . . . [but there is a need] to identify those clients who do or may present a risk to vulnerable others in order to maintain professional standards which do not value an abuser's therapeutic needs over his victim's needs for safety.

Some of the methods used

The practice methods employed by the Everyman Centre are also instructive. Apart from a 'participation contract' and an extensive 'suitability risk assessment schedule' taking part in counselling intervention involves exercises covering a number of topics/issues, including:

- 'time out': a form of contract that the perpetrator and his partner have agreed to as a way of helping her to feel safe, and him to calm down and think over issues looked at during counselling (a technique in wide use in relation to what is often called 'anger management'). The process also involves learning how to discharge pent up energy; relaxation; 'positive self-talk' (as an antidote), analysis, response and evaluation

- an assignment in which the perpetrator learns to recognise critical warning signs (or 'high-risk self states'), which may be physical, mental or behavioural—symptoms and which can remind the perpetrator that he is in danger of responding violently and of what may happen if he does not take action soon. These he must 'get to know like the back of his hand', including:

—*early signs:*
> **body:** e.g. tiredness, loss of appetite, poor sleep
> **feeling:** e.g. stress, resentment, bored, insecure, worried, unloved, inadequate
> **thought:** e.g. dwelling on old hurts, victim statements: 'Why does she do this to me?'
> **Action:** e.g. irritable, withdrawn, sulking, can't sit still, raised voice

—*late signs:*
> **body:** e.g. tense, tapping fingers, increased heart rate, shakiness, clammy hands
> **feeling:** e.g. powerless, anxious, panic, jealousy, angry
> **thought:** e.g. harbouring hatred, blaming, plotting revenge
> **action:** e.g. pacing up and down, standing too close, grinding your teeth, swearing, staring

—*very late signs:*
> **body:** e.g. tight chest, fist or jaw; shortness of breath, nausea, hot face, jumpiness, agitation
> **feeling:** e.g. helpless, angry, enraged
> **thought:** e.g. aggressive self-statements 'No one does this to me!'
> **action:** e.g. hand-waving, chasing, making threats.

The perpetrator is encouraged not only to recognise these high and low risk indicators but to take time out (above) and to practice positive self-talk and to recognise those particular self-statements that help to calm him down.

- an abuse questionnaire

- learning about the relationship in question, including 'a common sequence to change', underlined by the warning that

Every time you are violent or aggressive or you abuse or harass your partner, you destroy any progress and limit chances of rebuilding your relationship by making trusting very difficult.

- identification of high risk circumstances, including victims, places, issues, days, times, actions, words

- denial (in its many forms) and taking responsibility.

These represent just some of the methods and techniques which are employed by the centre which are set into a further background of experience and expertise in the causes, triggers and potentially sound responses to the specific problem of domestic violence.

A WISE INVESTMENT

In drawing this book to a close it seems apposite to return once more to words of Baroness Jay, the minister for women, with whose assertions about the importance of tackling domestic violence we opened our first chapter—but this time as reported at the launch of yet another initiative, the Newham Social Services report, *A Cry in the Dark: Children and Domestic Violence:*[26]

> The financial cost of assisting women (in fewer cases men) and children to be speedily and suitably rehoused, provided with benefits, health services, changes of school and immigration status amongst other services will not be cheap. Men left behind will also need services, including immediate advice and access to counselling, anger management programmes, and rehousing if the mothers and children are to return. In the long run this wise investment may break the cycle of violence in the home and greatly enhance the welfare of children within families. The current high costs of civil and criminal proceedings, criminal investigations, the penal system and other publicly funded responses is, arguably, poor value for money.

It now seems clear that government *is* prepared to make that 'wise investment' both (to an extent) in financial terms and in terms of encouraging the effective management of the local situation. It will also be considering the recommendations of the Advisory Board on Family Law concerning contact between children and parents or guardians where there has been domestic violence.[27] Indeed, this chapter—and the remainder of this book—indicates just how far attitudes towards and concern about domestic violence have advanced generally in a few short years—if at present mainly among those practitioners who are on the leading edge of developments. This is likely to accelerate as the various initiatives come together and the law itself begins to impact more decisively. This will not answer the primary question 'Why did violence

---

[26] Newham Social Services, 1999.

[27] See *A Consultation Paper on Contact Between Children and Violent Parents: The Question of Parental Contact Where there is Domestic Violence*, Advisory Board on Family Law, London, 1999, some further details of which appear at the end of *Appendix II*. The paper summarises the legal position and deals *inter alia* with 'Proposed Guidelines for Good Practice'.

occur in the first place?' (as to which we may need to look to deeper instincts) but it is well-worn ground that changes in attitudes and changes in behaviour are mutually reinforcing—and it is this that many of the strategies now being put in place are designed to influence.

No court or other decision-maker can purport to get it right all the time, especially when accurate prediction of risk is so difficult. What is certain is that everyone concerned to prevent domestic violence and who seeks to ensure the safety of women and children learns from everyone else involved in that process. Ultimately, it is a question of judgement and experience as to what level of risk is justified in any given situation and what is the best course of action, programme, initiative or sentence at that particular point in time. The broader the knowledge of the decision-maker and the more an 'integrated group' is contributing to this process, the wiser the investment—and the better everyone's judgement in these matters is likely to be.

Appendix I Form of Application for an Emergency Protection Order and Emergency Protection Order

Form of Application for an Emergency Protection Order in Respect of a Child

Supplement for an application for
an Emergency Protection Order
Section 44 Children Act 1989

Form C11

The court

The full name(s) of the child(ren)

1 Description of the child(ren)
If a child's identity is not known, state details which will identify the child. You may enclose a recent photograph of the child, which should be dated

2 The grounds for the application
The grounds are

A. ANY APPLICANT

☐ That there is reasonable cause to believe that [this] [these] child[ren] [is] [are] likely to suffer significant harm if

☐ the child[ren] [is] [are] not removed to accommodation provided by or on behalf of this applicant; **or**

☐ the child[ren] [does] [do] not remain in the place where [the child] [they] [is] [are] currently being accommodated.

B. LOCAL AUTHORITY APPLICANTS

☐ that enquiries are being made about the welfare of the child[ren] under section 47(1)(b) of Children Act 1989 **and** those enquiries are being frustrated by access to the child[ren] being unreasonably refused to someone who is authorised to seek access **and** there is reasonable cause to believe that access to the child[ren] is required as a matter of urgency.

C. AUTHORISED PERSON APPLICANTS

☐ that there is reasonable cause to suspect that the child[ren] [is] [are] suffering, or [is] [are] likely to suffer, significant harm **and** enquiries are being made with respect to the welfare of the child[ren] **and** those enquiries are being frustrated by access to the child[ren] being unreasonably refused to someone who is authorised to seek access and there is reasonable cause to believe that access to the child[ren] is required as a matter of urgency.

3 The additional order(s) applied for

☐ *Information on the whereabouts of the child[ren] (Section 48(1) Children Act 1989).*

☐ *Authorisation for entry of premises (Section 48(3) Children Act 1989).*

☐ *Authorisation to search for another child on the premises (Section 48(4) Children Act 1989).*

4 The direction(s) sought

☐ *Contact (Section 44(6)(a) Children Act 1989).*

☐ *A medical or psychiatric examination or other assessment of the child[ren] (Section 44(6)(b) Children Act 1989).*

☐ *To be accompanied by a registered medical practitioner, registered nurse or registered health visitor (Section 45(12) Children Act 1989).*

☐ *An exclusion requirement (Section 44A(1) Children Act 1989).*

5 The reason(s) for the application

If you are relying on a report or other documentary evidence, state the date(s) and author(s) and enclose a copy.

Signed   Date
(Applicant)

Emergency Protection Order

Form C23

In the   Court

Case Number:

Child(ren)'s Number(s):

Order   Emergency Protection Order
Section 44 Children Act 1989

The full name(s) of the child(ren)   Boy or Girl   Date(s) of birth

[described as

Warning: It is an offence intentionally to obstruct any person exercising the power under Section 44(4) Children Act 1989 to remove, or prevent the removal, of a child (Section 44(15) Children Act 1989).

The Court grants an Emergency Protection Order to the applicant who is

The Order gives the applicant parental responsibility for the child[ren].

The Court authorises

[the applicant to remove the child[ren] to accommodation provided by or on behalf of the applicant]

[the applicant to prevent the child[ren] being removed from

[This order directs that any person who can produce the child[ren] to the applicant must do so.]

The Court directs that [[a named person] be excluded from [a named address] [forthwith] [from[date]] so that the child may continue to live there, consent to the exclusion requirement having been given by [a named person]]

[a power of arrest be attached to the exclusion requirement for a period of]

This order ends on   at   [am] [pm]

Ordered by [Mr] [Mrs] Justice
[His] [Her] Honour Judge
District Judge [of Family Division]
Justice[s] of the Peace
On   at   [am] [pm]

Notes about the Emergency Protection Order

About this order
This is an Emergency Protection Order. The order states what has been authorised in respect of the child[ren] and when the order will end. The court can extend this order for up to seven days but it can only do this once.

Warning: If you are shown this order, you must comply with it. If you do not, you may commit an offence. Read the order now.

What you may do
You may apply to the court to change the directions or to end the order.

You may apply at any time, but the court will only hear an application to end an order when 72 hours have passed since the order was made.

If you would like to ask the court to change the directions, or end the order, you must fill in a form. You can obtain the form from a court office.

If the court has directed that the child[ren] should have a medical, psychiatric or another kind of examination, you may ask the court to allow a doctor of your choice to be at the examination.

What you should do
Go to a solicitor as soon as you can.

Some solicitors specialise in court proceedings which involve children. You can obtain the address of a solicitor or advice agency from the Yellow Pages or the Solicitor's Regional Directory. You will find these books at

- a Citizens Advice Bureau
- a Law Centre
- a local library

A solicitor or an advice agency will be able to tell you whether you may be eligible for legal aid.

Appendix II Welfare Considerations with Regard to Children

Chapter 2 contains an outline of the protections available in respect of children under the general law and by way of special statutory provision, in particular care orders or supervision orders. Care proceedings may be brought at the instigation of either a local authority or the NSPCC (*public law*) or a parent or guardian (e.g. with regard to contact with or the residence arrangements for a child) (*private law*). A court can only consider whether to make a care order if first satisfied:

(a) that the child concerned is suffering, or is likely to suffer, significant harm; and
(b) that the harm, or likelihood of harm, is attributable to:
    the care given to the child, or likely to be given to him if the order were not made, not being what it would be reasonable to expect a parent to give him; or the child being beyond parental control.

These are the 'threshold criteria' (sometimes called 'grounds'). They do not in themselves justify a care or supervision order, but are the minimum requirements before the court can go on to consider whether, in all the circumstances, it ought to make such an order. The court must, in particular, have regard to the welfare principle in section 1 of the 1989 Act (below). *Chapter 2* also outlines emergency protection orders (see also *Appendix 1*) — to deal with any immediate threat to a child — a range of other, less common orders and the existence of informal mechanisms designed to protect children such as local 'At-risk' registers usually maintained under the auspices of the local authority social services department.

Ever since the Children and Young Persons Act 1933, *all* courts (i.e. *criminal* or *civil*) where children appear — in whatever capacity — must have regard to their welfare. Section 44 of the 1933 Act provides:

Every court in dealing with a child or young person who is brought before it, either as an offender or otherwise, shall have regard to the welfare of the child or young person, and shall in a proper case take steps for removing him from undesirable surroundings, and for securing that proper provision is made for his education and training.

Additionally in relation to family matters to which the Children Act 1989 applies, section 1 of that act stipulates that:

* the child's welfare is the paramount consideration
* the court should not make an order unless it considers that to do so would be better for the child than making no order at all; and
* the court should have regard to the general principle that delay in determining a question with respect to the upbringing of a child is likely to prejudice the welfare of the child.

The philosophy of welfare
Other important messages can be gleaned from the 1989 Act, legal rulings, reports and discussion papers as follows:

- wherever possible, children should be brought up and cared for within their own families and by both parents
- parents with children 'in need' (including disabled children) should be helped to bring up their children themselves.

The support offered to a child and his or her family should:

- be provided *in partnership* with his or her parents
- meet the child's identifiable needs
- be appropriate in terms of the child's race, culture, religion and linguistic background
- draw on effective collaboration between the various agencies, including those in the voluntary sector
- ensure that children are safe, and protected by intervention if in danger (albeit that intervention must be open to challenge)
- provide adequate standards of care and high-quality substitute parenting if a child has no parents, or when parents cannot offer this themselves
- involve consulting and listening to the child and keeping him or her informed about what is happening to them
- safeguard contact with parents and the child's wider family who have a role in their children's lives, even when they live apart from them.

The welfare checklist

The 1989 Act provides a 'checklist'. In most *public law* (and contested *private law*) cases, section 1(3) states that the court must have regard, in particular, to:

(a) the ascertainable wishes and feelings of the child concerned (considered in the light of his age and understanding);
(b) his physical, emotional and educational needs;
(c) the likely effect on him of any change in his circumstances;
(d) his age, sex, background and any characteristics of his which the court considers relevant;
(e) any harm which he has suffered or is at risk of suffering;
(f) how capable each of his parents, and any other person in relation to whom the court considers the question to be relevant, is of meeting his needs;
(g) the range of powers available to the court under [the 1989] Act in the proceedings in question.

The Family Court Welfare Service

The Family Court Welfare Service operates under the auspices of the Probation Service. The principle tasks of the court welfare officer (CWO) in the present context are, at the request of the court:

- to meet the parties before or during a directions appointment for preliminary assessment and to identify areas of agreement

- to meet the parties at the direction of the court to assist them to make agreed decisions about their children
- to carry out enquiries and prepare a welfare report to assist the court.

The Home Office, in consultation with the Lord Chancellor's Department, the Department of Health and the Welsh Office, has issued National Standards for Probation Service Family Court Welfare Work which are designed to ensure consistency, fairness and good practice and that everyone dealing with CWOs is clear what to expect. The standards state that:

> the primary objective of all family court welfare work undertaken by the probation service is to help the courts in their task of serving the needs of children whose parents are involved in disputes in private law.

Mediation

Mediation and its sensitivity in relation to domestic violence is mentioned in *Chapter 8*. This process involves the parties in *privileged* discussions with a third party (the mediator) in an attempt to resolve disputes, in the present context, over the welfare of children. Mediation discussions *are* privileged (contrast e.g. a CWO's initial out of court discussions with the parties: above) which means that anything said may only be reported to the court if all parties to the proceedings involved in the discussions agree. There is an exception where, during mediation, something is said which indicates a risk of serious harm to the child — which would, of course, include domestic violence or other forms of child abuse.

Welfare reports

Section 7 Children Act 1989 provides that when the court is considering 'any question with respect to a child' under the 1989 Act, the court may ask a probation officer (i.e. usually the CWO) or an officer of the local authority (a social worker) to report to the court on any matters relating to the welfare of that child. The purpose of a welfare report is to provide the court with information which will enable it to make decisions which are in the best interests of the child. Normally the report is in writing except in situations where there is a verbal addendum or information is urgent.

Courts often have local agreements setting out which agency should respond to the request for a welfare report, but as a general rule the CWO deals with the majority of such requests in *private law* disputes unless there is some special reason to request otherwise.

Although the report writer should help the parties to reach agreement if he or she sees an opportunity for this during his or her inquiries, it is not the role of the CWO to set out to resolve disputes when preparing a report. Rather, the purpose is to inquire professionally and impartially.

The CWO will require a period in which to complete his or her inquiries and a date by which he or she should file the report with the court is given as a direction. Periods vary around the country (and with the nature of the case) from eight weeks up to 26 weeks. However, National Standards indicate that the report should be filed within ten weeks of receipt of the papers by the Family Court Welfare Service.

To ensure that the nature and scope of the inquiries match the circumstances of the case and reflect matters which the court wants to see dealt with, courts have been requested to adopt a pro forma. A Best Practice note has also been issued to all court staff.

Welfare reports are *confidential* to the court and, in compliance with National Standards (below), should be endorsed:

> This report has been prepared for the court and should be treated as confidential. It must not be shown nor its contents revealed to any person other than a party or a legal advisor to such a party. Such legal advisor may make use of the report in connection with an application for legal aid.

The completed report is sent to the court which then releases copies to the parties' legal representatives. If a party is not legally represented then either the report is sent direct to him or her or he or she is asked to come to the court office to read it.

National Standards for welfare reports

National Standards set out how information should be gathered by the CWO, for example, by seeing the parties together or separately, visiting them at home, seeing the child. The standards point out that inquiries should be even-handed and fair to both parties.

Checks are made via the local authority Child Protection Register (the 'At-risk' register': above), probation records and the police.

The report should deal with all relevant matters in the 'welfare checklist' (above). In particular, the wishes and feelings of any child should be reported to the court unless there are strong grounds for not doing so, when the reasons for that should be reported. If it becomes apparent to the CWO in the course of his or her inquiries that a child may be at risk of significant harm (e.g. domestic violence and sex abuse), then this should be reported immediately to the police and social services in accordance with local child protection procedures. The court will be advised and issue directions accordingly.

The guardian *ad litem*

The need for an independent voice to speak for children in care proceedings was first recognised by the Committee of Inquiry into the death of Maria Colwell in 1974 (which also led to the practice of keeping local 'At-risk' registers). The application to discharge the care order in that case was unopposed and the committee stated: 'It would have been of assistance to the court to have had the views of an independent social worker.'

Nowadays, in most *public law* cases, the justices' clerk or the court must appoint a *guardian ad litem* to safeguard the child's interests, unless satisfied that this is not necessary. In practice, guardians are appointed in over 98 per cent of cases.

Separate representation

The child's solicitor and guardian will usually work side by side and quite amicably, but differences of opinion can arise where the child is mature enough to take a different view to the guardian and wishes to instruct the solicitor direct. The rules provide that the guardian must inform the court of any such disagreement and then act and participate in the proceedings as directed. They also provide for independent legal representation for the guardian in such a situation. The guardian may, with the leave of the justices' clerk or the court, have legal representation 'in his or her conduct of those duties'.

National Standards

National Standards for guardians were published by the Department of Health and the Welsh Office in 1995. The standards confirm, e.g. that:

- in each case under the Children Act 1989, the guardian ensures that the welfare of the child is the paramount consideration;
- full consideration is given to ascertaining the wishes and the feelings of the child; and among many other practice requirements that
- the investigation is undertaken in general in a competent manner.

'Significant harm'

The Children Act 1989 criteria use the term 'significant harm'. Mere harm is not enough. Harm is defined as ill-treatment or impairment of health or development (concepts then further defined to include, for example, sexual abuse, emotional abuse and neglect). The Act does not define the word 'significant' but case law indicates that the ordinary dictionary definition applies. Further, when

> ... the question of whether harm suffered by a child is significant turns on the child's health or development, his health or development shall be compared with that which could reasonably be expected of a similar child.

Not only must 'significant harm', or its likelihood, be established, but also that the harm is attributable to a failure of reasonable parental care or that the child is beyond parental control.

Plans for the child

The local authority will also need to tell the court about its own plans for the child if an order were to be made. This will be relevant to the child's welfare and whether an order should be made. In relation to contact by people with the child, before making a care order the court must:

- consider the arrangements the authority has made, or proposes to make, for affording any individual contact with the child; and
- invite the parties to comment on those arrangements.

Supervision orders

Subject to the same threshold criteria set out above, the court can make an order placing a child under the supervision of the local authority or a probation officer.

Most orders are supervised by local authority social workers. A child may only be placed under the supervision of a probation officer if the local authority so request, and a probation officer is already exercising, or has exercised, in relation to another member of the household, duties imposed on it by statute. The duty of the supervising officer is to:

- advise, assist and befriend the child
- take such steps as are reasonably necessary to give effect to the order; and
- where the order is not wholly complied with, or the officer thinks it is no longer necessary, to consider applying for a variation or discharge.

Child contact and domestic violence

A Consultation Paper on Contact Between Children and Violent Parents: The Question of Parental Contact in Cases Where there is Domestic Violence has been issued by the Children Act Sub-Committee of the Advisory Board on Family Law. The paper surveys existing law and practice relating to 'the problem of domestic violence involving, or in the presence of, children and its relevance to contact disputes' and examines the competing interests brought about by the desirability of children remaining in touch with their natural parents wherever possible and appropriate. It quotes the legal test as '. . . are there any cogent reasons why the father should be denied access to his children? or, putting it another way: are there cogent reasons why . . . children should be denied the opportunity of access to their natural father?' (*Re H (Minors) (Access)* [1992] 1 FLR 148, per Lord Justice Balcombe). Clearly, domestic violence can constitute 'cogent reasons', but there is also the possibility of contact occurring subject to pre-conditions (the paper mentions a violent father seeking medical advice or psychotherapy or attending an anger management course) and the terms of any contact arrangements allowed by a court can also be structured so as to minimise the risk of future harm. Nonetheless, there is a delicate balance to be struck and as indicated by *Re M (Minors) (Contact: Violent Parent)* [1999] 2 FCR 56, 68 where the High Court dismissed a father's appeal against the refusal of magistrates to make a contact order, saying:

> Often in these cases where domestic violence has been found, too little weight . . . is given to the need for the father to change. It is often said that notwithstanding the violence the mother must nonetheless bring up the children with full knowledge and a positive image of their natural father and arrange for the children to be available for contact. Too often, it seems . . . the courts neglect the other side of that equation which is that a father . . . must demonstrate that he is a fit person to exercise contact; that he is not going to destabilise the family; and that he is not going to upset the children and harm them emotionally.

The report of the Children Act Sub-committee of the Advisory Board on Family Law is due later in 1999, including views on 'Proposed Guidelines for Good Practice' and upon information, monitoring and research.

Index

Introduction to the
Family Proceedings Court

Elaine Laken
Chris Bazell
Winston Gordon

With a Foreword by Sir Stephen Brown

Edited by Bryan Gibson

This highly readable account contains a basic outline of the law and practice of the family proceedings court in England and Wales as produced under the auspices of the Justices' Clerks' Society for use by family panel magistrates and other people interested in the arrangements for local justice for children and families.

CONTENTS

A competence based resource from the Waterside Introductory Series

ISBN 1 872 870 46 5 £13.50 per copy